D1312683

THE
ILLUSTRATED
FLAG
HANDBOOK

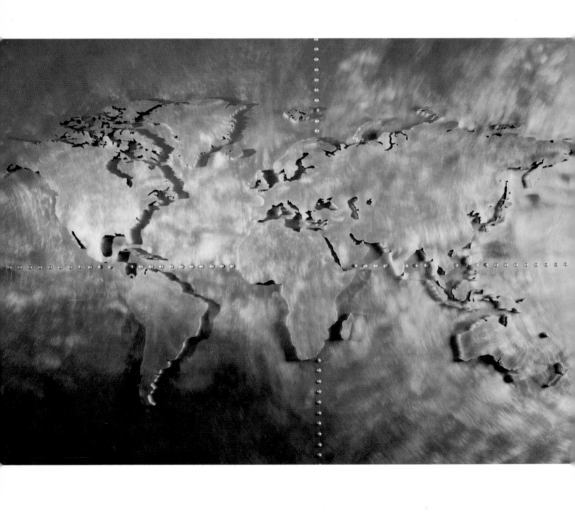

THE ILLUSTRATED FLAG HANDBOOK

M A R I A   C O S T A N T I N O

GRAMERCY BOOKS - NEW YORK

This 2001 edition is published by Gramercy Books™, an imprint of Random House Value Publishing, Inc., 280 Park Avenue, New York, NY 10017, by arrangement with D&S Books, Cottage Meadow, Bocombe, Parkham, Bideford, Devon, England, EX39 5PH.

Gramercy Books™ and design are trademarks of Random House Value Publishing, Inc.

Printed in Singapore.

Random House
New York • Toronto • London • Sydney • Auckland

A catalog record for this title is available from the Library of Congress

ISBN: 0-517-21810-0

987654321

Flag images © Flag Institute Enterprises, Maps © Photodisc 2001

Contents

Introduction 7

Glossary 22

An A–Z of Flags .26

International Flags 225

U.S. State Flags .241

Canadian Province Flags 254

Introduction

People across the world have used flags and banners in a variety of shapes, styles, and colors for more than 5,000 years. Flags were probably first used in wars to identify the warring parties, but they were no doubt also used in religious ceremonies.

The first flaglike objects were vexilloids, solid emblems in the shape of birds or abstract symbols that were carried high atop poles. Because they pointed upward, toward the heavens, it seems that these vexilloids were invested with mystical powers that were believed to protect their owners and bring them victory. Although the Roman legions used vexilloids in the shape of eagles, the Romans were also the first to use cloth banners.

Heraldic Flags

The designs of most modern flags originated in the Middle Ages and were derived from the heraldry – the distinctive coats of arms – of kings and lords. Some of these coats of arms appear on modern flags, but because they are quite complex in their original form (and have a whole vocabulary of heraldic terms to describe them), many modern flags feature simplified versions.

A motif that appears on many flags is the cross. This was the symbol that was used to unite the various European peoples who fought in the Crusades in the Holy Land during the 12th and 13th centuries. While this is an appropriate symbol for Christians, other religions, such as Islam, Judaism, or Buddhism, may use other emblems that express their faith.

Switzerland

National Flags

National flags are a relatively recent development. As you read through the accompanying text for each flag, you will notice that a great many nations only emerged in their modern form during the 18th, 19th, and 20th centuries – more new nations will probably be created in future.

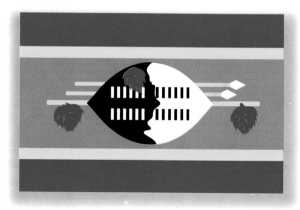

Swaziland

Ghana

Many of the flags used today evolved from nationalist and revolutionary movements, and you will find several flags that are related in design to the Dutch *Prinsenvlag,* an orange, white, and blue tricolor that was first used in The Netherlands at around 1600, when the Dutch were fighting for their independence from Spain. A tricolor flag gained even greater significance when, in red, white, and blue, it became associated with the French Revolution of 1789.

With the growth of independent states, flags have become important as political tools. Many newly independent states have selected national flags that are based on the design or colors of the political parties that secured the nation's independence. Other modern flags owe their design to the earlier flags of the federations of which they were members. Many of the Central American nations, for example, have flags based on the flag of the United Provinces of Central America, which was formed in 1823. The flags of many modern Arab states are based on the Arab Revolt flag of 1917 or the flag of the Egyptian Liberation Movement (1953), while a number of African nations have chosen flags in Pan-African colors derived from the flags of Ethiopia and Marcus Garvey and made popular by Ghana.

Symbolic Colors

Albania

The colors used on modern flags are often symbolic and it is important to remember that the meaning of colors may change from culture to culture. Red has traditionally been the color associated with socialism, but can also symbolize the struggle of a nation for independence. In Islamic cultures, green is considered the color of the Prophet Mohammed and is used to proclaim the country's faith. In this book, if a color has a specific meaning or association, the flag's entry endeavors to account for it.

The shape, proportions, colors, arrangement, and emblems of flags are generally enshrined in each nation's laws, and there are protocols or rules that govern their use. In the United States, for instance, the "Stars and Stripes" cannot dip in salute and should never be allowed to touch the ground. If it does, it must be replaced with a new one and the "soiled" flag be properly disposed of, for example, by giving it to the American Legion, who will make sure that it is treated with honor.

The "Union Jack," on the other hand, has never officially been enshrined in law as the national flag of the United Kingdom! It is strictly a royal standard that has become Britain's national flag through repeated use. At sea, however, the Union Jack is the official flag of the British Royal Navy, as well as the flag of rank for an admiral of the Fleet. Consequently, it is illegal for a civilian ship to fly this flag, which must instead use the "Red Duster" Civil Ensign (a red field with a Union Jack in the canton - see p12). Government vessels must use the Blue Ensign and naval vessels the White Ensign.

Some flags take precedence over others. When a national flag is flown with the flag of the United Nations, for instance, the U.N. flag takes precedence. The presence of the International Committee of the Red Cross, signified by the Red Cross flag and the Red Crescent flag, must be observed and acknowledged, misuse of these symbols being deemed a war crime.

All national flags are symbols of a nation's identity and ideals. It is a common courtesy to treat another nation's flag with the same respect that you would expect your own flag to be shown.

Parts of the Flag

CANTON, strictly means any quarter of the flag's field; most commonly it refers to the upper quarter nearest the staff

CHARGE, an emblem placed in the field or added to the basic design of the flag

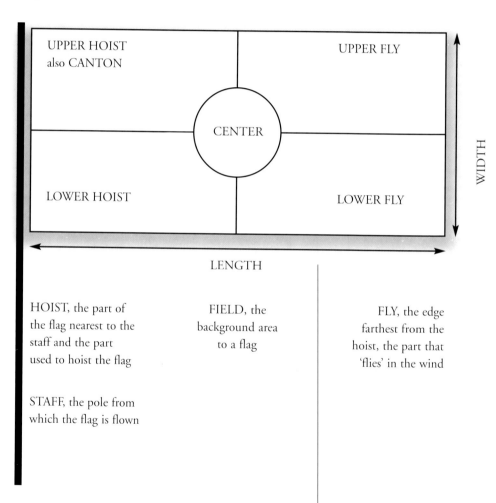

UPPER HOIST
also CANTON

UPPER FLY

CENTER

LOWER HOIST

LOWER FLY

WIDTH

LENGTH

HOIST, the part of the flag nearest to the staff and the part used to hoist the flag

FIELD, the background area to a flag

FLY, the edge farthest from the hoist, the part that 'flies' in the wind

STAFF, the pole from which the flag is flown

A flag of two strips of different colors arranged horizontally or vertically

Indonesia

Algeria

Triband

A flag of two colors in three bands arranged horizontally or vertically

Barbados

Austria

A flag of three colors in three bands arranged horizontally or vertically

Belgium

Afghanistan

Cross

A cross is vertically and centrally placed with the 'arms' extending across
the whole field

England

A cross with the upright 'arm' set closer toward the hoist

Finland

A diagonal cross stretching from corner to corner

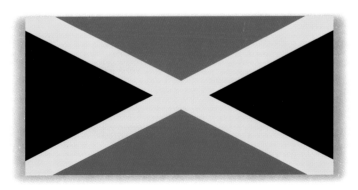

Jamaica

Couped Cross
and Couped Saltire

Couped describes a cross or
saltire with the ends cut short

Switzerland

Counterchanged

A charge placed on a line where
two colors meet, which reverses
them

United Kingdom

A flag where two colors are separated by a serrated edge

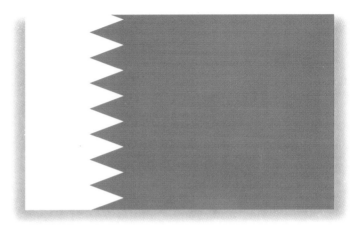

Bahrain

A narrow strip or edge of color that separates broader stripes or larger areas of color

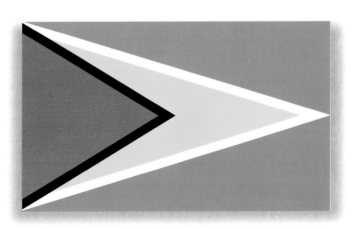

Guyana

Triangle

Djibouti

A flag divided by a triangle of a different color, most often at the hoist

Bordered

Grenada

A flag where the central color is bordered by a different color

A flag quartered into four equal parts, each of an alternating or different color, or design

Dominican Republic

GLOSSARY

Arms Arms are the heraldic symbols of a nation or family. They include a shield bearing distinctive colors and devices (designs), supporters (human, animal, or mythical figures) on either side of the shield, a crest (an heraldic symbol) above the shield, and sometimes other insignia. Arms often appear on flags in simplified form, and sometimes only the shield is used.

Bicolor A bicolor is a flag consisting of two bands of color. The bands can be arranged horizontally or vertically.

Bordered When a flag is bordered, the central color on a flag is surrounded by a different color. For examples, see Maldives (page 131) and Sri Lanka (page 190).

Canton A canton means a quarter of the area of the flag (or shield). On a flag, it is generally on the upper left-hand corner.

Charge A charge is the figure, symbol, or *emblem* in the *field* of a flag.

Civil flag A civil flag is the *national flag* that is used by private citizens on land.

Counterchange A counterchange is when the position of two colors on either side of a line are reversed. See, for example, the flag of the United Kingdom (page 212), on which the crosses of St. Andrew and St. Patrick have been counterchanged.

Emblem An emblem is a device that is often used as *charge* on a flag, but can also be used separately. Emblems may represent a nation or city, or even a family or organization.

Ensign An ensign is the national flag that is flown at the stern of ships. A country may have a civil ensign for use on passenger and merchant ships, a state ensign for use on nonmilitary vessels, and a naval ensign for use on warships.

Field The field is the background of a flag (or shield).

Fimbriation Fimbriation is a narrow edging or border added to a colored area or stripe on a flag in order to separate it from the adjoining area or color.

Fly The fly is the outer edge of a flag, the part that "flies" in the wind and is farthest away from the flagpole.

Hoist The hoist is the edge of the flag nearest to the flagpole. The word is also used as a verb, "to hoist" meaning to raise a flag.

Jack A jack is a small flag flown on a ship's bow (front) to show its nationality.

Length The length is the measurement of the flag along the side that is at a right angle to the flagpole.

Obverse Obverse means the front side of the flag, the side that is visible when the *hoist* is on the viewer's left. See also *reverse*.

National flag A national flag is the same as a *civil flag*. National flags are the familiar flags that are used internationally, but can be different from *state flags*.

Pennant A pennant is a small, tapering or triangular flag, used for signaling a ship's identification. Civil flags in this form are often used as souvenirs or decorations. The civil flag of Nepal (page 147) is unique in its shape, formed as it is from two pennants.

Provincial flag In addition to a national flag, many countries also have individual state, province, or territory flags. The United States, for example, has the "Stars and Stripes" (page 213) as its national flag, 50 state flags, and flags for self-governing dependencies, such as American Samoa, Guam, the U.S. Virgin Islands, Puerto Rico, and the Northern Mariana Islands. Canada flies the "Maple Leaf Flag" (page 57) as its national flag, but also uses the Canadian Red Ensign (with the Union Jack in the canton), while each Canadian province flies its own flag. Such flags are illustrated in this book.

Quartered When a flag is said to be quartered, it has been divided into four equal sections, each of which may be plain or decorated. For examples, see Panama (page 160) and Dominican Republic (page 76).

Ratio A flag's ratio is its proportions, described as its width relative to its length. For each flag, you will find the official proportions expressed as a ratio. For example, the flag of Canada (see page 57) has a ratio of 1:2, which means that the width of the flag is two times the length.

Reverse A flag's reverse is the "back" or "wrong" side of a flag when the flagpole is on the viewer's right.

Saltire A saltire is a cross with diagonal arms that stretch from corner to corner of the flag.

Serration Serration describes a flag in which two colors are separated by a serrated (zigzag) edge. See Bahrain (page 39) and Qatar (page 167).

State flag A state flag is the *national flag* flown on land by government and official organizations. Unlike a *civil flag,* a state flag usually carries the national *arms.* The flags illustrated in this book are all civil flags.

Triangle A triangle describes when a flag is divided by a triangle of a different color, usually at the *hoist.* For examples, see Bahamas (page 38), Sudan (page 191), and Cuba (page 70).

Triband Triband describes a flag in two colors that are arranged in three bands, either vertically or horizontally. For examples, see Austria (page 36), Latvia (page 119), and Nigeria (page 152).

Tricolor A tricolor is a flag of three bands in three different colors. The bands can be arranged either vertically or horizontally. For examples, see France (page 87), Germany (page 91), and Colombia (page 63).

Vexillology Vexillology is the study of flags and their history. The word is derived from the Latin *vexillum,* which was a square flag used by the Roman cavalry. A vexilloid is an *emblem* that can either be solid – like the standard of a Roman legion – or of cloth, such as a flag.

If you are interested in becoming a vexillologist, someone who studies flags and their history, there are many vexillological societies and associations across the world that you could join. Their governing body, the International Federation of Vexillological Associations (F.I.A.V.), has its headquarters in Houston, Texas, and London, U.K., as well as its own flag. F.I.A.V. organizes regular conferences about flags, covering their history, use, design, and development. Search the Internet for your local flag association, which should give you more details of how to join, as well as links to other flag sites.

Width A flag's width is its measurement along the side that is parallel to the flagpole.

In the following A-Z directory of flags, each flag is accompanied by a low-scale map showing the general location of the relevant country.

AN
A–Z
OF
FLAGS

AFGHANISTAN

Formal name:
Dowlat-e Eslami-ye Afghanestan
(Islamic State of Afghanistan)

Capital city:
Kabul

Location:
South Central Asia

Currency:
1 Afghani = 100 puls

Languages:
Pushtu, Dari (Persian)

Religions:
Sunni Muslim, Shi'ite Muslim

Flag adopted:
December 2, 1992

Flag ratio:
1:2

In 1973, the royal kingdom established in Afghanistan in 1926 was overthrown and a republic declared. A period of internal unrest and political instability was followed by a Soviet-backed coup and invasion from 1979 to 1989. In 1992, the *Mujaheddin* ("Holy Warriors") seized power and adopted the green, white, and black tricolor, with a gold coat of arms, as its national flag.

The black stripe recalls the flags used by Afghanistan in the past, while green is the regarded as the "color of the Prophet" and represents the Islamic faith. The coat of arms shows a mosque encircled by a wreath of wheat ears placed within two crossed swords. Between the tips of the wheat ears is the *shahada*, the Muslim confession of faith. Below are the words *Allahu Aqbar* ("God is Great") and, at the bottom of the wreath, the name "Islamic State of Afghanistan." Directly above this is the Muslim date 1371, said to correspond to the year A.D. 1992, the date of the *Mujaheddin* victory.

Note
This is the national flag currently recognized by the United Nations. Since 1996, the Talibaan *(fundamentalist Islamic theologists and their students) have gained control of the capital Kabul, as well as much of the country. Should the* Talibaan *become the legitimate rulers of Afghanistan, a new administration may change the existing flag or adopt a new one.*

ALBANIA

From the 4th century A.D. until 1347, Albania was part of the Byzantine Empire, after which followed decades of invasions by Bulgarians, Serbs, Venetians, and, in 1385, Turks. The fight for independence was led during the 1440s by George Castriota, (1403–68), also known as Skanderberg or Iskander Bey, an Albanian Christian and former Turkish general. In 1443, Skanderberg first hoisted a red flag bearing the figure of a double-headed eagle (in Albanian, the country's name, *Shqipërisë,* means "land of the eagle"). In 1478, Albania became part of the Ottoman Empire.

Independence was gained in 1912, and the red flag bearing the eagle was officially adopted. Albania declared itself a republic in 1925, but in 1928 President Ahmed Beg Zogu was proclaimed King Zog. During World War II, Albania was overrun by Germany and Italy (and parts of the Italian arms were added to the flag). Although the original flag was restored in 1942, in 1946 Albania became a republic ruled by a strict communist government, who added a gold-fimbriated, red star representing the communist regime to the flag. In 1991, free, multiparty elections were held and the new Albanian government ordered the removal of the star, returning the flag to its form of 1912.

Formal name:
Republika e Shqipërisë
(Republic of Albania)

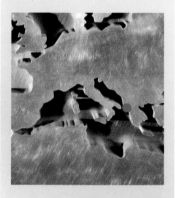

Capital city:
Tirana

Location: Southeast Europe

Currency:
1 lek = 100 qindars

Language:
Albanian

Religions:
Christian, Sunni Muslim

Flag adopted:
April 7, 1992

Flag ratio:
5:7

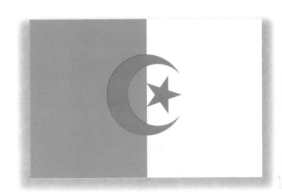

Formal name:
Al Jumhuriyah al Jaza'iriyah ad
Dimuqratiyah ash Shabiyah
(Democratic and Popular
Republic of Algeria)

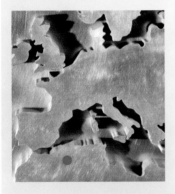

Capital city:
Al Jaza'ir (Algiers)

Location:
Northwest Africa

Currency:
1 Algerian dinar
= 100 centimes

Languages:
Arabic, Berber

Religion:
Sunni Muslim

Flag adopted:
July 3, 1962

Flag ratio:
2:3

During the 18th century, Algeria was a thriving base for pirates, and, on the pretext of protecting its trade and ships, in 1830 France invaded the country. By 1860, much of Algeria was under French control. In 1954, the *Front de Libération Nationale* (F.L.N.) began an uprising that turned into a bitter war which finally ended in 1962, when Algeria gained its independence.

Many believe that the Algerian flag is a variation of the flag of the liberation forces that was originally created in 1928. It was subsequently adopted by the F.L.N. and used as the flag of the provisional government in exile from 1958 to 1962. When independence was achieved, this flag, constituted by a green and white rectangle embossed with a red star and red crescent, was formally adopted. The green of the hoist represents the traditional color of Islam, while the white of the fly symbolizes purity. The star and crescent are recognized symbols of Islam, and red represents the blood of the national heroes of liberation. The horns of the crescent, which are longer than usual, represent good fortune and prosperity.

ANDORRA

Formal name:
Principat d'Andorra
(Principality of Andorra)

Declared a free state by the Holy Roman Emperor Charlemagne during the 9th century, in 1278 the principality of Andorra came under the joint sovereignty of a spiritual "prince," the Spanish bishop of Urgel, and a temporal (earthly) "prince," originally the count of Foix, whose title passed to the French head of state in 1589. In 1993, the principality's once fragile democracy adopted a constitution that gave the country virtual independence, admission to the United Nations, and the safeguarding of its external security by France and Spain.

To the existing flag of yellow and red, adopted in 1866, Andorra now added a blue field. France and Spain thus being represented by two colors each: red and blue for France and red and yellow for Spain. In the middle of the central yellow stripe is the Andorran coat of arms. The emblems on the quartered shield represent Andorra's traditional protectors; a bishop's miter and crosier signifying the bishop of Urgel and three vertical red stripes symbolizing the counts of Foix. Catalonia is represented by four red stripes on a yellow ground, and Bearn, a province of southwest France, by a pair of cows. These refer to the arms of the Counts of Bearn who were involved in the historical French rule of the region along with the Counts of Foix. Beneath the shield is the motto *Virtus Unita Fortior* ("United Strength is Greater").

Capital city:
Andorra-la-Vella

Location:
Southwest Europe (between France and Spain)

Currency:
French franc, Spanish peseta

Languages:
Catalan, French, Spanish

Religion:
Roman Catholic

Flag adopted:
1866

Flag ratio:
2:3

Formal name:
República de Angola
(Republic of Angola)

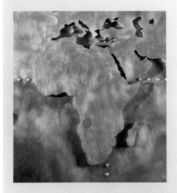

Capital city:
Luanda

Location:
Southwest Africa

Currency:
1 new kwanza = 100 lwei

Languages:
Portuguese, Bantu

Religions:
Roman Catholic, Animist

Flag adopted:
November 11, 1975

Flag ratio:
2:3

The Kongo and Ndongo kingdoms ruled much of the area that is now Angola when the Portuguese arrived in 1491 to develop both a colony and slave trade. After centuries of foreign domination and repression, a liberation movement was started in 1956 by the People's Movement for the Liberation of Angola (M.P.L.A.). The M.P.L.A. was succeeded by two further nationalist movements: the National Front for the Liberation of Angola (F.N.L.A.) and the National Union for the Total Independence of Angola (U.N.I.T.A.). Political protest led to guerrilla war in 1961, independence from Portugal being finally achieved in 1975, although civil war and guerrilla action between rival factions has continued.

The present national flag of Angola is similar to that used by the ruling M.P.L.A. in 1975, but with the addition of a yellow star to symbolize communism and internationalism. Horizontally bicolored, the upper red stripe signifies the blood shed in the struggle for liberty, while the lower black stripe symbolizes Africa. A half cog wheel and machete, which were clearly inspired by the hammer and sickle of the Soviet flag, were also added as emblems of industry and agriculture. The yellow color of the central emblems is said to represent Angola's rich mineral resources.

ANTIGUA & BARBUDA

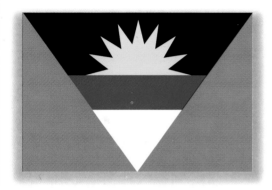

Formal name:
Antigua and Barbuda

This independent, tropical-island state consists of three Leeward Islands: Antigua, Barbuda, and the rocky, uninhabited island of Redonda. Christopher Columbus was the first European to visit Antigua in 1493, although he did not go ashore. Antigua remained uncolonized until 1632, when the British established a settlement, and Barbuda was colonized by Antiguan settlers in 1661. In 1967, Antigua and Barbuda was made a self-governing state, with Britain remaining responsible for its defense and foreign affairs. Full independence was granted on November 1, 1981, when Antigua and Barbuda became an independent state.

The national flag dates from 1967, when self-government was achieved, and is the result of a competition won by Reginald Samuel, a high-school art teacher. The design features two red, outer triangles, which symbolize the dynamism of the people, the triangles together forming a "V"-shape, which stands for victory. The golden-sun motif represents the dawn of a new era as it rises against the black ground that symbolizes the African ancestry of the people. The blue stripe signifies the waters of the Caribbean Sea, while the white represents the sands of the island's shores, also signifying hope.

Capital city:
St. John's

Location:
Eastern Caribbean

Currency:
1 East Caribbean dollar
= 100 cents

Language:
English

Religion:
Protestant

Flag adopted:
February 27, 1967

Flag ratio:
2:3

Formal name:
República Argentina
(Argentine Republic)

Capital city:
Buenos Aires

Location:
South America

Currency:
1 peso = 100 centavos

Language:
Spanish

Religions:
Roman Catholic, Protestant

Flag adopted:
February 12, 1812

Flag ratio:
1:2

The second-largest country in South America, the Argentine Republic occupies most of the southern portion of the continent. Originally inhabited by Native American peoples, Argentina was once part of the Inca civilization. It was first visited by Europeans during the early 16th century, the capital city, Buenos Aires, being founded in 1536. Having been made a Spanish viceroyalty in 1776, in 1810 the Argentinean populace revolted against Spanish rule. Full independence was achieved in 1816, although the war of liberation continued until 1820.

The blue and white colors of the national flag are those adopted by the revolutionary leader General Manuel Belgrano (1770–1820), who is said to have been inspired by looking at the sky. These colors were used to distinguish the Liberation Army from Spanish troops (who wore red insignia). On May 25, 1810, crowds of people wearing blue-and-white cockades massed in Buenos Aires to demand independence, and it is said that on this day the white clouds parted to reveal a blue sky and shining sun, heralding a bright future for a new nation. The golden "Sun of May" charge, with 32 alternating straight and flaming rays, was added to the blue-and-white flag in 1818.

ARMENIA

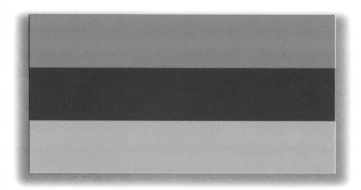

Formal name:
Hayastani Hanrapetut'yun
(Republic of Armenia); informal
name: Hayasta

In A.D. 300, Armenia became the first nation to proclaim
Christianity its official religion. Having been acquired by Russia
in 1828, following the fall of the czarist regime, an independent
Armenian state emerged for a brief period between 1918 and
1922. Armenia then became part of the Transcaucasian Soviet
Republic, and, in 1936, a separate union republic within the
U.S.S.R. As a result of Soviet premier Mikhail Gorbachev's
encouragement of *glasnost* ("openness"), Armenian national identity was reawakened and the republic declared its independence
from the U.S.S.R. on August 23, 1990. The new nation received
international recognition when the U.S.S.R. was dissolved in
December 1991 to be replaced by the Commonwealth of
Independent States (C.I.S.). In March 1992, Armenia became a
member of the United Nations.

Following Armenia's independence, the Soviet flag, which
depicted a hammer and sickle on a red field, was replaced by the
flag of the independent Armenia of the 1920s, a tricolor of red,
blue, and orange (although the original flag's ratio was 2:3). The
flag's colors are deeply symbolic: the red represents the blood
shed by Armenians, the blue symbolizes both the sky and hope,
and the orange denotes the land, as well as the Armenian
people's hard work and courage.

Capital city:
Yerevan

Location:
Eastern Europe

Currency:
1 dram = 100 looma

Languages:
Armenian, Azerbaijani, Russian

Religion:
Christian (Armenian Apostolic
Church)

Flag adopted:
August 24, 1990

Flag ratio:
1:2

Formal name:
Commonwealth of Australia

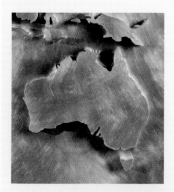

Capital:
Canberra

Location:
Oceania

Currency:
1 Australian dollar = 100 cents

Languages:
English, Aboriginal languages

Religions:
Anglican, Roman Catholic,
diverse others

Flag adopted:
May 22, 1909

Flag ratio:
2:1

Situated between the Pacific and Indian oceans, the country of Australia entirely occupies the Earth's smallest continent. Although Aboriginal peoples have lived there for some 40,000 years, the first recorded sighting of Australia by Europeans was only made in 1606. Captain James Cook having proclaimed New South Wales a British colony in 1770, the first flag flown on Australian soil was the "Union Jack."

From 1778 the Union Jack remained Australia's national flag, that is, until the six formerly separate British subject states (South Australia, Victoria, New South Wales, Queensland, Tasmania, and Western Australia) were unified as the Commonwealth of Australia on January 1, 1901. In that year, a competition was held to search for a new flag, the judging committee eventually deciding on a design that incorporated aspects of six entries. The Union Jack continues to occupy the canton, emphasizing Australia's continued links with the U.K., and beneath it is the Commonwealth Star, which originally had six points, each representing one of the six states, the seventh being added in 1909 to represent the Northern Territory. In the fly are the five white stars of the Southern Cross constellation that is visible in southern night skies throughout the year. The four larger stars have seven points, while the smallest star has five.

AUSTRIA

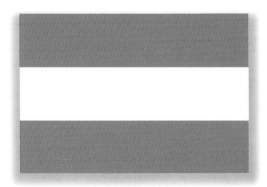

Formal name:
Republik Österreich
(Republic of Austria)

In ancient times, the inhabitants of this land-locked, mountainous country were Celtic tribes. In 14 B.C., the country to the south of the River Danube was conquered by the Romans, the region being occupied by Vandals, Goths, Huns, Lombards, and Avars after the fall of the Roman Empire until A.D. 791, when Charlemagne, the Holy Roman Emperor, established the foundations of the Austrian Empire.

The region was ruled by the Babenberg family from the 10th century to 1250, and legend states that during the Battle of Acre in 1191, the white surcoat worn by the Crusader Luitpold V of Babenberg became so bloodied that the only part that remained white was underneath his sword belt. Thus it was that red, with a white band across, became both Luitpold and Austria's colors and remained an emblem of Austria for over 900 years, making this flag one of the world's oldest. Austria officially adopted the flag in 1918, when it became a republic following the overthrow of the last Hapsburg emperor. During World War II, when Austria was invaded by Hitler's troops and incorporated into the German *Reich*, the Austrian flag was banned. With the conclusion of the war in 1945, however, the flag was restored.

Capital city:
Wien (Vienna)

Location:
Central Europe

Currency:
1 schilling = 100 groschen

Language:
German

Religions:
Roman Catholic, Protestant

Flag adopted:
May 1, 1945

Flag ratio:
2:3

Formal name:
Azarbaycan Respublikasi
(Azerbaijani Republic)

Capital city:
Baku

Location:
Eastern Europe

Currency:
1 manat = 100 gopik

Languages:
Azerbaijani (Turkish), Russian

Religion:
Shi'ite Muslim

Flag adopted:
February 5, 1991

Flag ratio:
1:2

Although it was conquered by the Arabs in A.D. 632 and remained under Arab control until the 11th century, Azerbaijan shares a common language and culture with its historic ally, Turkey. Before Azerbaijan was conquered by czarist Russian forces during the early 19th century, it was a province of Persia. Today, some 20 million Shi'ite Azeris live across the border in Iran. A member of the Transcaucasian Federation in 1917, with Turkish support, Azerbaijan enjoyed a brief period of independence between 1918 and 1920 before then being occupied by the Bolshevik Red Army and becoming part of the U.S.S.R. in 1922.

The national flag used today dates back to Azerbaijan's independence and replaced the hammer and sickle of the Soviet flag in 1991. Consisting of three wide, horizontal stripes, the colors of the flag represent the Azerbaijani motto to "Turkify, Islamicize, and Europeanize," the uppermost blue stripe signaling an affinity with Turkic peoples, the central red stripe representing development, and green being the traditional color of Islam. The white crescent and star is similar to the charge on the Turkish flag, the eight-pointed star symbolizing the different branches of the Turkish people.

THE BAHAMAS

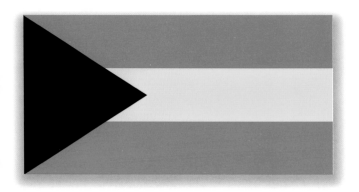

Formal name:
Commonwealth of the
Bahamas

Extending for about 750 miles (about 1,200 kilometers) from a point southeast of Palm Beach, Florida, to a point off the eastern tip of Cuba, the Bahamas comprise an archipelago of some 700 islands (only 30 of which are inhabited), plus more than 2,000 cays and rocks. The subtropical Bahamas were first reached by Christopher Columbus, who landed at San Salvador (Watling) in 1492. In 1647, the British established permanent settlements at Eleutheria and New Providence before giving the islands to the duke of Albermarle as a proprietary colony three years later. Until the Bahamas reverted to the British crown in 1717, the islands were a haven for pirates, most notably the infamous Blackbeard. In 1782, during the American War of Independence, Spanish forces captured the islands, but returned them to the British in 1783. Today an independent state, the Bahamas achieved internal autonomy in 1964 and independence in 1973.

The design for the new national flag was based on the winning entry in a competition held following the attainment of independence. The blue is intended to represent the aquamarine seas surrounding the islands, while the yellow symbolizes their golden sands. The black triangle in the hoist denotes the African heritage of the Bahamian people, as well as their unity and strength.

Capital city:
Nassau

Location:
North Atlantic/Caribbean

Currency:
1 Bahamian dollar = 100 cents

Language:
English

Religion:
Protestant

Flag adopted:
July 10, 1973

Flag ratio:
1:2

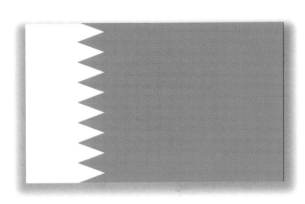

Formal name:
Dawlat al-Bahrain
(State of Bahrain)

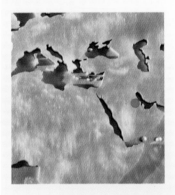

Capital city:
Al Manamah (Manama)

Location:
Middle East

Currency:
1 Bahrain dinar = 1000 fils

Language:
Arabic

Religions:
Sunni Muslim, Shi'ite Muslim

Flag adopted:
August 19, 1972

Flag ratio:
3:2

Bahrain is made up of 33 islands on the western side of the Persian Gulf. Part of the Arab Islamic world since the 7th century, during the 17th century Bahrain was ruled by the Persians until 1783, when the rule of the Sunni al-Khalifa family, which continues to this day, was established. A series of 19th-century treaties led to Bahrain becoming a British protectorate, and because piracy was a problem in the Gulf and Britain was keen to defend its shipping routes, in 1820 the General Maritime Treaty asked that all states on friendly terms with Britain display white in their flags. To distinguish its plain flag, in the traditional red color of the Kharijit Muslims of Eastern Arabia, Bahrain therefore added a plain, white, vertical stripe to the hoist.

Britain announced the ending of its protectorate in 1968. Bahrain then briefly joined Qatar and the Trucial States (now the United Arab Emirates) to form the Federation of Arab Emirates. In 1971, however, Bahrain left the federation and became an independent state. The national flag's modern form dates from 1932, when the line between the white and red was serrated to distinguish it from the flags of Ajman, Abu Dhabi, and Dubai.

BANGLADESH

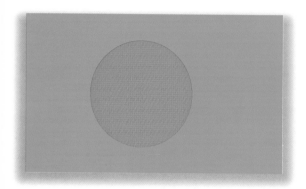

Formal name:
Gana Praja-tantri Bangladesh
(People's Republic of
Bangladesh)

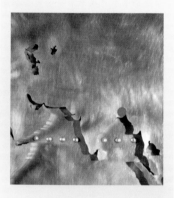

Capital city:
Dhaka (Dacca)

Location:
Asia

Currency:
1 Bangladesh taka = 100 poisha

Languages:
Bengali, English

Religions:
Muslim, Hindu

Flag adopted:
January 13, 1972

Flag ratio:
3:5

Part of the Mogul Empire from the 16th century, the area that today comprises Bangladesh came under the British rule of India from 1757, when it was known as East Bengal. After Partition in 1947, the area became an eastern province of Pakistan, its designation changing to East Pakistan in 1955. The largely Muslim eastern province, which was separated from the politically dominant, Urdu-speaking West Pakistan by 1,000 miles (1,600 kilometers) of India, resented the domination exerted upon it. Resentment led to civil war, and on March 26, 1971 the region declared its independence as Bangladesh (the Bengali word for "Free Bengal"), with full independence being gained in December 1971.

The first flag adopted by Bangladesh in March 1971, during the struggle for independence, consisted of a green field with a golden map of Bangladesh contained within the center of a red disk. The current flag, adopted in December 1971, omits the map – some say that it was an unpleasant reminder of the partition of Bengal. The green field represents the fertility of the land, the vigor of the people, and the importance of Islam. The plain, red disk, set slightly off-center toward the hoist (so that it can be clearly seen when the flag flutters) symbolizes the country's struggle for independence.

Formal name:
Barbados

Capital city:
Bridgetown

Location:
Caribbean

Currency:
1 Barbados dollar = 100 cents

Language:
English

Religion:
Protestant

Flag adopted:
November 30, 1966

Flag ratio:
2:3

Just 21 miles (34 kilometers) long and 14 miles (23 kilometers) wide at its broadest part, Barbados is the easternmost island of the West Indies. Originally inhabited by the Arawak people, who were wiped out soon after the arrival of the first Europeans, Barbados derives its name from the Portuguese *Os Barbados*, the name for the bearded fig trees that at one time covered the island. Barbados was claimed and settled by the British in 1627, the island remaining a British colony until independence was achieved in 1966.

The design for the national flag, like many other flags of the Caribbean nations, was the result of a competition won by Grantley Prescod, an art teacher. The blue and gold stripes represent the seas and sand that surround the island. The trident in the middle is both the emblem of the Roman sea god, Neptune (reflecting the importance of the sea to Barbados) and is also derived from an earlier flag-badge which depicted Britannia holding a trident, the emblem of British rulership of the seas. In Prescod's design, the trident shaft is broken, symbolizing the island's break with its colonial past. The points of the trident today represent the three principles of democracy: government of, for, and, by the people.

BELARUS

A Belarussian state developed during the Middle Ages, chiefly around the town of Polotsk on the River Dvina. During the 13th century, Belarussia became part of the Grand Duchy of Lithuania before being joined with Poland in 1569 and then incorporated into the Russian Empire during the late 18th century. An upsurge in national consciousness began to manifest itself during the late 19th century, and in 1918, during the Bolshevik Revolution, Belarussia declared itself an independent republic, although it failed to win international recognition. As a result, it was established as the Belarussian Soviet Socialist Republic in 1919, one of the four founding republics of the U.S.S.R. Following the dissolution of the U.S.S.R., on August 25, 1991, Belarussia proclaimed its independence, in September of the same year voting to change its name to "Republic of Belarus."

The flag adopted in 1991 was of three stripes arranged in the order white-red-white, the traditional colors of *Belyj Rus* ("White Russia"). On May 14, 1995, however, a referendum was held to determine whether Belarus should strengthen its ties with Russia, which also included a proposal for a new national flag. Endorsed by the people, the new white, green, and red flag resembles the Belarussian flag that was flown when Belarussia was part of the U.S.S.R. (albeit without the hammer, sickle, and star emblems of communism), and in the design on the hoist ornamentation (which represents a traditional woven cloth), the red and white have been reversed.

Formal name:
Respublika Belarus,
(Republic of Belarus)

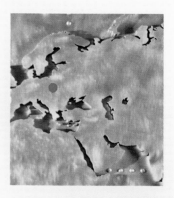

Capital city:
Minsk

Location:
Eastern Europe

Currency:
1 rouble = 100 kopeks

Languages:
Belarussian, Russian, Polish

Religions:
Roman Catholic, Russian Orthodox

Flag adopted:
May 6, 1995

Flag ratio:
1:2

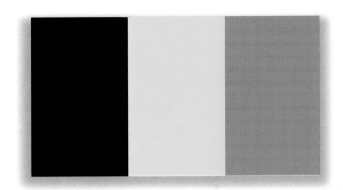

Formal name:
Royaume de Belgique (French)
Koninkrijk België (Flemish)
(Kingdom of Belgium)

Capital city:
Bruxelles (Brussels)

Location:
Western Europe

Currency: euro,
1 Belgian franc = 100 centimes

Languages:
French, Flemish (Dutch),
German

Religion:
Roman Catholic

Flag adopted:
September 3, 1831

Flag ratio:
13:15

Conquered by the Romans in 15 B.C., and then by the Franks during the 3rd century A.D., during the 9th century the region that we now know as Belgium was the prosperous center of the lands of the Holy Roman Emperor Charlemagne. During the 15th century, the Belgian counties came under the rule of the French dukes of Burgundy, later, by means of a series of marriage alliances, falling under the rule of first the Hapsburg Empire and then Philip II of Spain, becoming part of the Netherlands in 1815. An uprising in 1830 led to the area known as the South Netherlands becoming recognized as the independent and permanently neutral kingdom of Belgium, under the rule of Leopold of Saxe-Coburg.

The black (hoist), yellow (middle), and red (fly) colors of the Belgian flag are said to be derived from the flag of the province of Brabant. A flag in these horizontally arranged colors was flown in 1789, when the Belgians unsuccessfully rose against the Hapsburgs. During the 1830 revolt against the Dutch king, William I, it is said that two men, Lucien Jottrand and Edouard Ducpetiaux, recalling the colors of the 1789 standard, recreated the horizontally striped, three-color flag. Following the pattern of the French *Tricolore*, the stripes were changed to their vertical position following Belgium's independence in 1830, although it maintained its almost square shape.

BELIZE

Once part of the Maya civilization, and colonized during the 17th century by English woodcutters from Jamaica, Belize was known as British Honduras until 1973. The country became self-governing in 1964, achieving full independence in 1981 (although British forces continued to maintain a defensive involvement until 1994).

During the period of its self-government, Belize adopted an unofficial flag of blue (the color of the People's United Party, P.U.P.), with the national coat of arms, which recall the country's predominant industry, logging – but without the British "Union Jack" on the canton of the shield – on a central white disk. The shield's top panels depict the tools of the logging industry, while below is a sailing ship, symbolizing trade. The supporting figures are Mestizo and Creole workers, representing the varied origins of Belize's people, behind whom stands the national tree and major economic resource, the mahogany. Underneath is the national motto *Sub Umbra Floreo* ("I Flourish in the Shade"), and surrounding all is a wreath of 50 leaves, recalling the year 1950, when the P.U.P. came to prominence. Although this flag was retained on Belize's attainment of independence in 1981, in recognition of the P.U.P.'s rival party, the United Democratic Party, two red bands were added to the design.

Formal name:
Belize

Capital city:
Belmopan

Location:
Central America

Currency:
1 Belize dollar = 100 cents

Languages:
English, Spanish

Religions:
Roman Catholic, Protestant

Flag adopted:
September 21, 1981

Flag ratio:
3:5

Formal name:
République du Bénin
(Republic of Benin)

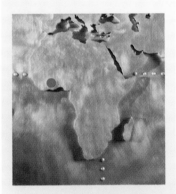

Capital:
Porto-Novo

Location:
Western Africa

Currency:
C.F.A. franc = 100 centimes

Languages:
French, local dialects

Religions:
Roman Catholic, Muslim,
Animist

Flag adopted:
November 16, 1959
(abandoned 1975, reintroduced
August 1, 1990)

Flag ratio:
2:3

A powerful kingdom since the 12th century, Dahomey (as the country was called until 1975) came under French influence during the 1850s, becoming part of French West Africa in 1899. In 1900, the rule of the last king, Ago Li Ago was overthrown, and the country became the French colony of Dahomey. Having become self-governing in 1958, in 1960 it achieved full independence as the Republic of Dahomey.

From 1959 to 1975, the flag that was flown was the same as the one in current use. While they are also Pan-African, symbolizing African unity and nationalism, the local significance of the flag's colors are explained in Benin's national anthem: the green of the hoist signifies hope and revival, while the red and yellow, horizontal stripes respectively represent the courage of ancestors and the country's wealth. In 1975, however, the flag, along with the country's name, was changed by the Marxist-Leninist Party of the People's Revolution of Benin, the national flag becoming a plain green field with a red communist star in the canton. Although the name Benin was retained, when the country abandoned socialism in favor of multiparty democracy in 1990, the tricolored flag was reintroduced.

BHUTAN

Formal name:
Druk-Gyal-Khab
(Kingdom of Bhután)

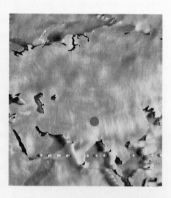

The name "Bhután" means "Land of the Thunder Dragon" in Dzongkha, the country's official language, which is based on Tibetan and uses *chhokey* (the Tibetan script) for writing. Ruled by Tibet from the 16th century, and then by China from 1720, during the late 18th century the eastern Himalayan country of Bhután came increasingly under the influence of Britain. Bhután's hereditary monarchy was established in 1907, and three years later the Anglo-Bhután Treaty granted the country internal autonomy, although its foreign relations continued to be controlled by the British government in India until Partition in 1947. Bhután is a Buddhist state, in which power is shared by the *druk gyalpo* ("Dragon King"), a council of ministers, and the *Tshogdu,* a semi-democratically elected national assembly.

In Bhután, the noise of thunder in the mountains is believed to be the roaring of dragons (*druk* means both "dragon" and "thunder"), and the "thunder-dragon" emblem appears on the national flag. The *druk* is white, symbolizing purity, and clutches jewels in its claws, representing the country's wealth. The field, which is divided diagonally, is of two colors. The upper portion, in saffron yellow, represents the secular authority of the ruling Wangchuk Dynasty, while the lower, red portion signifies Buddhist spiritual authority.

Capital city:
Thimphu

Location:
Asia

Currency:
1 ngultrum = 100 chetrums

Languages:
Dzongkha, Nepali, English

Religions:
Buddhist, Hindu

Flag adopted:
1969

Flag ratio:
2:3

Formal name:
República de Bolivia
(Republic of Bolivia)

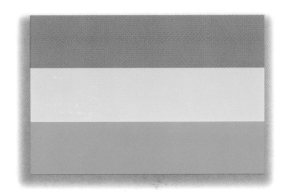

Capital city:
La Paz

Location:
South America

Currency:
1 Bolivian peso = 100 centavos

Languages:
Spanish, Quechua, Aymara

Religion:
Roman Catholic

Flag adopted:
October 31, 1851

Flag ratio:
2:3

Nicknamed the "Rooftop of the World" because of its elevated position in the Andes Mountains, Bolivia was part of the Inca civilization before being conquered by Spain in 1538. Then known as Upper Peru, it remained under Spanish rule until liberated in 1825 by the nationalist and revolutionary leader Simón Bolívar, after whom the modern nation was named. (Bolívar had already liberated his native Venezuela (in 1821), Colombia and Ecuador (in 1822), and Peru (in 1824) from Spanish rule.)

The Bolivian flag of 1825 consisted of three horizontal bands in the order red-green-red, with five golden stars within laurel wreaths. In 1826, the order of stripes was altered to yellow (top), green (middle), and red (bottom), in the center of which were placed the arms. The flag was altered in 1851 to the flag that is in current use. The order of the stripes were again changed, and now run red, yellow, and green. The red is symbolic of the blood shed in the struggle for independence, as well as Bolivia's courage, the yellow represents the country's rich mineral wealth, while the green signifies its natural fertility and agriculture.

BOSNIA & HERZEGOVINA

Formal name:
Bosna i Hercegovina
(Bosnia and Herzegovina)

Once an ancient Roman province, the area that is today known as Bosnia-Herzegovina was incorporated into the Yugoslav Socialist Federal Republic in 1945. In 1990, nationalist parties routed the ruling communists in the elections, but conflict between Serbia and Croatia – and civil war in the latter – spread chaos into Bosnia-Herzegovina. A referendum in 1992 showed that a majority was in favor of Bosnian independence from Yugoslavia, international recognition of Bosnia-Herzegovina being gained in April 1992. The country is now divided into two parts: the Bosnian-Croat Federation and the Serb Republic.

When Bosnia-Herzegovina seceded from Yugoslavia in 1992, and at a time when the three leading ethnic groups (Muslims, Serbs, and Croats) were at war with each other, the first flag adopted by the new nation was a neutral, white field bearing the central blue, white, and gold shield of the Kotromanic Dynasty (the last independent rulers of the country during the 14th century). This flag was unacceptable to some factions, however, and in 1998 a new flag, designed by a committee of members from all three ethnic groups, was adopted. The colors of blue, white, and gold having been retained, a gold triangle represents the country's shape, as well as the three ethnic groups. The continuous stars were inspired by the European Union flag and represent peace and the future.

Capital city:
Sarajevo

Location:
Central Europe

Currency:
1 konvertibilna = 100 pfeniga

Languages:
Bosnian, Croatian, Serbian

Religions:
Muslim, Serbian Orthodox,
Roman Catholic

Flag adopted:
February 4, 1998

Flag ratio:
1:2

Formal name:
Republic of Botswana

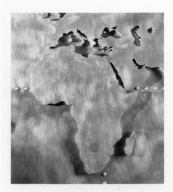

Capital city:
Gabarone

Location:
Southern Africa

Currency:
1 pula = 100 thebe

Languages:
English, Setswana

Religions:
Christian, diverse indigenous
beliefs

Flag adopted:
September 30, 1996

Flag ratio:
2:3

The first inhabitants of the region now known as Botswana were the Kung, hunter-gatherers who lived chiefly in the Kalahari Desert. During the 17th century, the Tswana people populated the area, followed by the Bantu people during the 19th century. Fearing invasion by Boer farmers, the rulers of the lands appealed to the British for support, and in 1885 the region consequently became a British protectorate known as Bechuanaland. Now known by its Setswana name of Botswana, in 1966 the country gained its independence without a struggle, thereupon adopting a blue, black, and white national flag.

Unusually, this flag is not derived from that of the dominant political party, nor does it feature the Pan-African colors of red, yellow, and green. Instead, the two horizontal blue bands represent *pula*, the life-giving rain that is vital to this arid land. (*Pula*, which means "Let there be rain," is also the motto on the arms of Botswana.) The black stripe, fimbriated with white in the center, symbolizes the racial harmony of the African and European citizens of Botswana and is said to have been inspired by the coat of Botswana's national animal, the zebra.

BRAZIL

Formal name:
República Federativa do Brasil
(Federative Republic of Brazil)

Brazil was colonized by the Portuguese after the explorer Pedro Alvares Cobral landed there in 1500 and was named after the red dyewood *pau brasil* (brazilwood), the first natural commodity to be exploited. In 1808, the French emperor Napoleon invaded Portugal, prompting the Portuguese king, John VI, to move his capital from Lisbon to Rio de Janeiro. He returned to Portugal in the following year, leaving his son, Crown Prince Pedro, in Brazil as regent; in 1822, Pedro assumed the title Emperor Pedro I and declared Brazil independent.

The green field and yellow lozenge of the Brazilian flag, which respectively represent the country's rainforests and vast mineral resources, and also refer to the royal houses of Braganza and Hapsburg, were part of the first flag to be adopted when independence was proclaimed. In 1889, the imperial arms were replaced by a view of the night sky as it appeared over Rio de Janeiro when the republic was formed, each of the stars in the constellations on the flag representing a state in the Brazilian federation. The number of stars has altered over time, and the latest version, formally adopted on May 11, 1992, contains 27. Brazil's national motto, *Ordem e Progresso,* ("Order and Progress") is emblazoned on a band across the center of the night sky.

Capital city:
Brasilia

Location:
South America

Currency:
1 real = 100 centavos

Language:
Portuguese

Religions:
Roman Catholic, Protestant

Flag adopted:
May 11, 1992

Flag ratio:
7:10

Formal name:
Negara Brunei Darussalam

Capital city:
Bander Seri Begawan

Location:
Southeast Asia

Currency:
1 Brunei dollar = 100 cents

Languages:
Malay, English

Religions:
Sunni Muslim, Buddhist,
Christian

Flag adopted:
September 29, 1959

Flag ratio:
1:2

An independent Islamic sultanate from the 15th century, by the 16th century the sultans of Brunei ruled all of Borneo and parts of the Philippines. By the 19th century, however, with its territory reduced, Brunei became a haven for pirates. From 1888 to 1971 Brunei was a British protectorate, self-government being followed by full independence in 1984, although under the alleged absolute rule of Muda Hassanai Bolkiah.

Brunei's flag evolved throughout the 20th century. Its base, a field of plain yellow, was the flag of the sultan, to which was added in 1906 two diagonal stripes – a broad, white stripe over a narrower black one – in recognition of the country's status as a British protectorate. The current flag also bears the coat of arms that was added in 1959, the year of Brunei's autonomy. The arms show a red *Bulan* (crescent), the traditional symbol of Islam, bearing the motto "Always Give Service by God's Guidance," below which are the words *Brunei Darussalam* "(Brunei, City of Peace")*. Between the tips of the crescent are the *Bendera* (flag) and *Payung Ubor-Ubor* (the royal umbrella), both symbols of royalty, which rest on the *Sayap* (wings of four feathers) that symbolize the protection of justice. To each side is a *Tingan* or *Kimhap* (an upraised hand), which represents the government's pledge to work for the people's welfare, peace, and prosperity.

BULGARIA

Formal name:
Narodna Republika Bulgariya
(Republic of Bulgaria)

Occupied by the Slavs during the 6th century, and then by the Bulgars during the 7th, during the 9th century Bulgaria, under the rule of the Eastern Christian Orthodox Czar Simeon (893–927), became a leading power in Southeastern Europe. From the 11th century, however, and for the next 500 years, Bulgaria was part of the Ottoman Empire. It became a principality in 1878 and an independent kingdom in 1908. The monarchy having been abolished in 1946, in the following year a Soviet-style constitution was adopted. The communist ruling powers collapsed in 1990, whereupon Bulgaria was redefined as a republic.

During Ottoman Turkish rule, Bulgaria had no national flag, but when it became a principality it adopted a tricolor flag based on the Russian flag at that time, but with a central, green stripe instead of a blue one (red, white, and blue are the Pan-Slavic colors). The top white band represents peace; the central green one symbolizes the youthfulness of the emerging nation; and the bottom red stripe denotes the courage of the Bulgarian people. With the formation of the People's Republic of Bulgaria in 1947, a coat of arms was added to the white stripe, near to the hoist, depicting a lion rampant, the red star of communism, and a cog wheel, symbolizing industry. Following the fall of communism in 1990, the arms were removed from the flag.

Capital city:
Sofiya (Sofia)

Location:
Eastern Europe

Currency:
1 lev = 100 stotinki

Language:
Bulgarian

Religions:
Orthodox Christian, Muslim

Flag adopted:
November 27, 1990

Flag ratio:
3:5

Formal name:
République de Burkina Faso
(Republic of Burkina Faso)

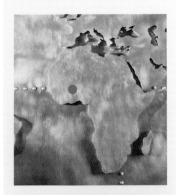

Capital city:
Ouagadougou

Location:
Western Africa

Currency:
1 C.F.A. franc = 100 centimes

Languages:
French, More, Gur (the ethnic languages of the Mossi and Bobo)

Religions:
Animist, Muslim, Roman Catholic

Flag adopted:
August 4, 1984

Flag ratio:
2:3

The area known since 1984 as Burkina Faso was formerly called Upper Volta. During the 1890s, it became a province of French West Africa until 1958, when it became a self-governing republic, full independence from France being achieved in 1960.

The flag adopted at this time contained three horizontal stripes of black, white, and red, which represented the three major tributaries of the River Volta that flows through the country. Following a series of coups, in 1984 it was announced by the ruling powers that the country would be renamed Burkina Faso. A combination of two ethnic groups' languages (the More language of the Mossi and the Gur language of the Bobo), Burkina Faso means "Land of Honorable Men," and its adoption symbolized a break with its colonial past. A new flag, in the colors of the Pan-African movement – red, green, and gold – was also adopted. The upper, red band symbolizes the 1984 revolution, the lower, green band, agriculture and the country's abundant natural resources, as well as its hope. The central, yellow, five-pointed star represents the country's riches and symbolizes the guiding light of the revolution.

BURUNDI

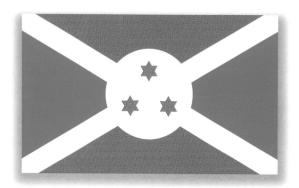

Formal name:
Republika y'u Burundi/République du Burundi
(Republic of Burundi)

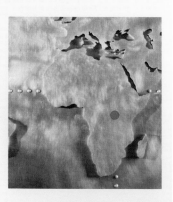

One of Africa's smallest countries, and originally inhabited by Twa pygmies during the 13th century, Burundi was overrun by Bantu Hutus while, from the 15th century, the Tutsi king ruled the area then known as Urundi. The country became part of German East Africa in 1890, before becoming a Belgian territory after World War I. Later, as part of Ruanda-Urundi, it was administered by Belgium as a League of Nations' (and subsequently United Nations') trust territory. Burundi achieved independence in 1962 and was ruled by King Mwambutsu until 1966, when he was deposed and a republic declared.

The flag that was adopted on Burundi's independence contained the emblem of a drum – denoting the ruling monarchy – as well as a sorghum plant, within a central disk. When the republic was declared, the drum was removed, however, the sorghum emblem also being removed a year later and replaced with three stars. Often said to represent the country's three ethnic groups, the Hutu, Tutsi, and Twa, the stars officially refer to the three words of the national motto: *Unité, Travail, Progrès* ("Unity, Work, Progress"). The colors are also symbolic: green represents hope, white signifies peace, and red symbolizes the blood shed in the fight for independence, first from Germany, and then from Belgium.

Capital city:
Usumbura (also known as Bujumbura)

Location:
Central Africa

Currency:
1 Burundi franc = 100 centimes

Languages:
French, Kirundi

Religion:
Roman Catholic

Flag adopted:
June 28, 1967

Flag ratio:
2:3

Formal name:
Reacheanachak Kampuchea
(Kingdom of Cambodia)

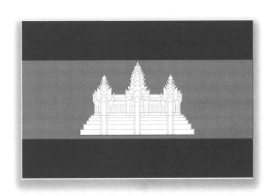

Capital city:
Phnom Penh

Location:
Southeast Asia

Currency:
1 riel = 100 sen

Language:
Khmer

Religions:
Buddhist, Hindu, Muslim

Flag adopted:
June 30, 1993

Flag ratio:
2:3

During the 9th century, Jayavaran II, the Khmer king, established the Angkor Empire that would dominate much of Southeast Asia for some 600 years. A French protectorate was established in 1863, continuing (apart from during World War II) until 1953, although the monarchy remained in nominal control. In 1955, King (now Prince) Norodon Sihanouk abdicated in order to lead a broad coalition government. He was overthrown in 1970, when the Khmer Republic was declared, which was in turn toppled by communist Khmer Rouge guerrillas under Pol Pot in 1975. In 1979, anti-Khmer Rouge forces overthrew Pol Pot's regime and established the People's Republic of Kampuchea. The new state of Cambodia abandoned socialism in 1989, the monarchy being restored in 1993 and the country's named being changed to the Kingdom of Cambodia.

Although five different flags have been used since 1948, the current flag is the one that was first officially adopted on October 29, 1948. All have featured a representation of Cambodia's most famous landmark, the 12th-century temple of Angkor Wat. In Khmer cosmology, the pedestal of the temple represents Mount Meru, the structure of the universe, while at the top of the temple is the sanctuary of Cambhu, the lord-creator of the world. The blue bands at the top and bottom of the flag symbolize Cambodian royalty, the central, red band represents the nation, and the white of the temple denotes Buddhism.

CAMEROON

Formal name:
*République du
Cameroun/Cameroon*
(Republic of
Cameroun/Cameroon)

In 1472, the Portuguese were the first Europeans to visit this West African country, which they named Camaro-es. In 1884, Germany declared a protectorate over Kamerun (as it was then called), after World War I France governing about 80 percent of the country under a League of Nations' mandate as French Cameroun, while Britain administered the remaining 20 percent, which became British Cameroons. In 1946, both regions became United Nations' trust territories, and in 1959 French Cameroun gained internal self-government, with full independence being granted in 1960. The following year, northern parts of the British Cameroons merged with Nigeria, while the south was federated with the former French territory.

The original flag adopted by the autonomous Cameroon in 1959 was based on the French *Tricolore,* but flew the Pan-African colors of green (hoist), red (middle), and yellow (fly). Cameroun was the second modern African state (after Ghana) to adopt these colors. In 1961, when the southern British Cameroons voted to join Cameroun, two yellow stars were added to the upper hoist to signify the two territories. After the Republic of Cameroun became a unitary state, however, one star was dropped and the single, remaining star was placed on the center of the flag that has today remained in use since 1975.

Capital city:
Yaoundé

Location:
West Africa

Currency:
1 C.F.A. franc = 100 centimes

Languages:
French, English, Bantu, diverse
tribal languages

Religions:
Christian, Muslim, diverse
indigenous beliefs

Flag adopted:
May 20, 1975

Flag ratio:
2:3

CANADA

Formal name:
Dominion of Canada

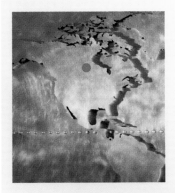

Capital city:
Ottawa

Location:
North America

Currency:
1 Canadian dollar = 100 cents

Languages:
English, French, Inuktitut

Religions:
Protestant, Roman Catholic

Flag adopted:
February 15, 1965

Flag ratio:
1:2

Although fully independent since 1931, Canada's sovereign is the British monarch. Modern Canada was formed by the confederation in 1867 of Ontario, Newfoundland, and Quebec, creating a partially independent state of provinces. Additional provinces – Alberta, British Columbia, Manitoba, New Brunswick, Nova Scotia, Prince Edward Island, and Saskatchewan – as well as three territories – Northwest Territories, Yukon, and Nanavut – have since joined the confederation to create the Dominion of Canada, the second-largest country in the world.

Until 1965, Canada did not have its own flag, instead flying the British Red Ensign with the Canadian arms on the fly. During the 1960s, however, public pressure for the country's own flag led to a design called the "Pearson Pennant," which featured a maple leaf, the Canadian national symbol for more than 150 years, with a blue bar on each side to represent the Pacific and Atlantic oceans. Although it did not meet with universal approval, a consensus emerged on the use of the maple-leaf symbol, as well as the national colors of red and white. Known informally as the "Maple Leaf Flag," or *L'Unifolie* (which means "one-leafed" in French), the final design was adopted in 1965. Although the British Union Jack continues to be flown in Canada, the Maple Leaf Flag takes precedence in all instances apart from during a royal visit.

CAPE VERDE

Formal name:
República de Cabo Verde
(Republic of Cape Verde)

First settled during the 15th century by the Portuguese, the first black inhabitants of the group of ten volcanic islands that make up Cape Verde were slaves transported from West Africa. Portugal ruled the islands for the next five hundred years and, although many inhabitants maintained their African culture, most became Roman Catholic and now speak Portuguese or the Portuguese-derived Crioulo (Creole). During the 1950s, a liberation movement emerged, the mainland West African territory of Guinea-Bissau (to which Cape Verde was linked, a federation of the two countries once being planned) achieving independence from Portugal in 1974. Cape Verde also gained its independence in 1975, whereupon it modeled its new flag on that of Guinea-Bissau, since both shared the same dominant political party, the *Partido Africano para a Independencia de Guine e Cabo Verde* (P.A.I.G.C.). The planned union with Guinea-Bissau was canceled in 1981, however, and Cape Verde abandoned the one-party political system.

In the wake of a new constitution, which was drawn up in 1992, Cape Verde jettisoned its original, green-red-yellow flag in favor of a new design. The new flag contains ten yellow stars representing the ten islands, the blue field symbolizing the sea in which they are set, while the horizontal, red line fimbriated with white signifies the islands' latitudinal location.

Capital city:
Praia

Location:
Atlantic Ocean, due west of the westernmost point of Africa

Currency:
I Cape Verdean escudo = 100 centavos

Languages:
Portuguese, Crioulo

Religion:
Roman Catholic

Flag adopted:
September 22, 1992

Flag ratio:
3:5

Formal name:
République Centrafricaine
(Central African Republic)

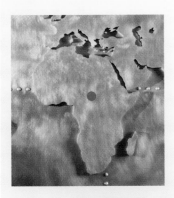

Capital city:
Bagui

Location:
West Africa

Currency:
1 C.F.A. franc = 100 centimes

Languages:
Sango, French, other diverse local dialects, and African languages

Religions:
Animist, Christian, Muslim

Flag adopted:
December 1, 1958

Flag ratio
3:5

A French colony from the late 19th century, the territory known as Ubangi-Shari became self-governing within French Equatorial Africa in 1958. It became the Central African Republic in 1960.

The national flag is an unusual – indeed, unique – design, since it uses both the Pan-African colors of red, yellow, and green and the national colors of France (red, white, blue), its former colonial ruler. Together, these colors symbolize the nation's ideals: freedom (blue), equality and purity (white), hope (green), and tolerance (yellow), while the red band that crosses the four horizontal colors vertically represents the blood that is common to both Europeans and Africans and symbolizes the need for mutual respect. The five-pointed yellow star set in the blue of the canton is interpreted as signifying the desire for African unity. The flag was adopted in 1958, at a time when it was hoped that neighboring French colonies would join a federation, and although this goal was never achieved, the design of the flag remained unaltered.

CHAD

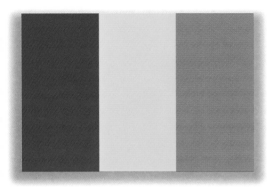

Formal name:
République du Tchad
(Republic of Chad)

When the region that is today known as Chad was first settled by the Arabs during the 7th century, it was called Kanem, being renamed Bornu on the establishment of an Islamic state during the 13th century. Conquered by Sudan during the 19th century, the area around Lake Chad subsequently fell to the French, whose domination of the country was completed by 1916. Part of French Equatorial Africa, Chad became an autonomous state within the French Community in 1958, achieving full independence in 1960.

Adopted in 1959, the flag of the Republic of Chad is modeled on the French *Tricolore*. Instead of the latter's red-white-blue arrangement, however, blue-yellow-red was chosen, two of the French national colors and two of the Pan-African colors popularized by Ghana thus being incorporated into the flag. The official symbolism of the colors of Chad's flag is as follows: blue represents the sky, hope, agriculture, and the southern part of the country; yellow denotes the sun and the northern desert lands; red signifies prosperity, unity, and the blood shed in the struggle for independence. Coincidentally, Chad's flag is the same as the one that is currently used by Romania.

Capital city:
N'djamena

Location:
West Africa

Currency:
1 C.F.A. franc = 100 centimes

Languages:
French, Arabic, Hausa, diverse other African languages

Religions:
Muslim, Christian, Animist

Flag adopted:
November 6, 1959

Flag ratio:
2:3

Formal name:
Républica de Chile
(Republic of Chile)

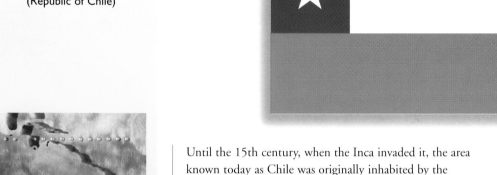

Capital city:
Santiago

Location:
South America

Currency:
1 Chilean peso = 100 centavos

Language:
Spanish

Religion:
Roman Catholic

Flag adopted:
October 18, 1817

Flag ratio:
2:3

Until the 15th century, when the Inca invaded it, the area known today as Chile was originally inhabited by the Auraucanician people. The first European to reach Chile was Ferdinand Magellan, who sailed through the strait now named after him in 1520. Members of a Spanish expedition under Pedro de Valdivia founded the capital, Santiago, in 1541, and Spanish settlement continued, despite the frequent rebellions of the native peoples. A revolution against Spanish rule was led by Bernardo O'Higgins in 1810, and in 1818, with the help of Argentinean troops led by José de San Martín, Chile was liberated from its colonial ruler.

While the French *Tricolore* became the model for the flags of many emerging European nations, in the New World that role was taken by the flag of the United States of America, and during the struggle for freedom from Spain, Chile adopted the red, white, and blue of the "Stars and Stripes." Although the design was initially a horizontal tricolor, in 1854 it was modified to form the present layout of two horizontal bands, white over red, with a blue canton charged with a white star. The blue represents the Andean sky, the white signifies the snow of the Andes, while the red denotes the blood of the patriots who died to win Chile's independence.

CHINA

Formal name:
Zhonghua Renmin Gongheguo
(People's Republic of China)

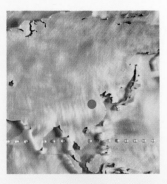

The world's largest country in terms of population, and also one of the largest in area, the Chinese call their country *Zhonghua*, which means "Middle Kingdom." The first historically documented dynasty to rule China was the Shang (from *c.*1480 to *c.*1050 B.C.), and from the 7th to the 14th century A.D. China enjoyed the world's most advanced civilization, influencing the cultural, technological, and political life of many other societies. China's political strength was eventually threatened by the expansion of various European empires: firstly by Portugal during the mid-16th century, and then by the British during the mid-19th century. Internal revolts weakened the last, Qing, dynasty, which was eventually overthrown by Chinese nationalists in 1911. Between 1927 and 1937, and 1946 and 1949, a civil war was fought between the nationalist and communist forces. Having been victorious in 1949, the Chinese Communist Party then established the People's Republic of China on the mainland (Taiwan remaining under the control of the nationalist Kuomintang).

The red flag of China was officially adopted on the same day that the republic was founded: October 1, 1949. The large, golden star in the canton of the red field represents the common program of the Communist Party, while the four smaller stars are said to represent the four classes that have been united by communism, that is, the workers, peasants, bourgeoisie, and "patriotic capitalists."

Capital city:
Beijing

Location:
Asia

Currency:
1 yuan = 10 jiao = 100 fen

Languages:
Putonghua (Mandarin Chinese, the official language), Cantonese, Shanghai-, Fukien-, Hakka- dialects, Tibetan, Vigus (Turkic)

Religions:
Confucian, Buddhist, Taoist

Flag adopted:
October 1, 1949

Flag ratio:
2:3

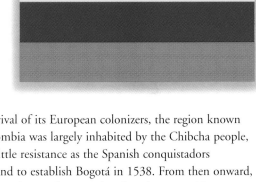

Formal name:
República de Colombia
(Republic of Colombia)

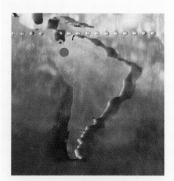

Capital city:
Bogotá

Location:
South America

Currency:
1 Colombian peso
= 100 centavos

Languages:
Spanish, plus numerous Indian dialects

Religion:
Roman Catholic

Flag adopted:
December 17, 1819

Flag ratio:
2:3

Before the arrival of its European colonizers, the region known today as Colombia was largely inhabited by the Chibcha people, who put up little resistance as the Spanish conquistadors advanced inland to establish Bogotá in 1538. From then onward, Colombia formed part of a Spanish colony known as New Granada, which comprised Colombia, Panama, and most of Venezuela. The area was enlarged in 1819 to include Ecuador, while in same year it gained its independence from Spain, the new state of Gran Colombia being established by "The Liberator," Simón Bolívar.

Like those of its neighbors, Ecuador and Venezuela, Colombia's flag was based on the flag flown by Bolívar's troops during the struggle for independence, the colors of which were first used by Bolívar's predecessor, Francisco de Miranda, in 1806. After Ecuador and Venezuela broke away from their union with Gran Colombia in 1830, Colombia continued to use the flag that it had adopted in 1819, although the stripes were arranged vertically until 1861. The double-width, yellow stripe, which dates from the days when Gran Colombia was first formed, symbolizes universal liberty and justice; the blue stripe represents the sea and skies surrounding the country; while the red stripe denotes fraternity and the blood shed by Colombia's liberators during their struggle for independence.

COMOROS

Formal name:
Jumhuriat Al-Qumur Al-Ittihadiyah Al-Islamiyah
(Federal Islamic Republic of the Comoros)

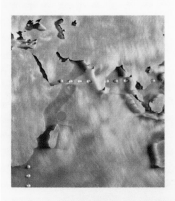

Capital city:
Moroni

Location:
India Ocean

Currency:
1 C.F.A. franc = 100 centimes

Languages:
French, Arabic

Religion:
Muslim

Flag adopted:
October 3, 1996

Flag ratio:
3:5

The four islands that constitute the Comoros were controlled by Muslim sultans until being acquired by the French in 1841. The islands became a French colony in 1912, from 1914 to 1947 being attached (for administrative purposes) to Madagascar. After this, the islands were made a French overseas territory, with internal autonomy being granted in 1961. Although three islands – Njazidja (Grande Comore), Nzwani (Anjouan), and Mwali (Molieli) – achieved full independence in 1975, the fourth island, Mayotte, voted to remain a French dependency.

Unlike many other former French territories, the Comoros did not adopt a variation on the French *Tricolore* following independence. The original flag of 1975 (which was mainly red, symbolizing the country's socialist ideals) was replaced in 1978 with a flag that paid tribute to the legacy of the island's Arab and Islamic culture in its field of green (the color of the Prophet Muhammad) and white crescent and stars. In 1996, the flag that remains current was adopted. The present flag bears the monograms of Allah (on upper part of the fly) and the Prophet Muhammad (on the lower part of the hoist), while placed between the horns of the crescent, facing toward the hoist edge, are four stars in a row, representing the four islands.

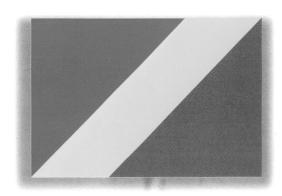

Formal name:
République du Congo
(Republic of the Congo)

Capital city:
Brazzaville

Location:
West Africa

Currency:
1 C.F.A. franc = 100 centimes

Languages:
French, Bantu

Flag adopted:
November 20, 1959

Flag ratio:
2:3

Before the arrival of the first Europeans during the 15th century, the region that is today the West African Republic of the Congo was inhabited by the Sanga, Bateke, and Bakongo peoples. In 1889, the Teke kingdom came under French protection, the region becoming the French colony of Middle Congo in 1905. Having become self-governing in 1958, full independence was achieved in 1960.

The current flag, which was originally adopted during the region's period of autonomy, bears the Pan-African colors of green, yellow, and red (making it the fifth national flag to use these colors), arranged diagonally from upper hoist to lower fly, with the yellow stripe narrower than the other portions. Although this flag was retained when independence was declared in 1960, following a Marxist revolution in 1969, a new flag was adopted when the country was renamed the People's Republic of the Congo. This flag was Soviet-inspired, with a red field. The hoist canton bore the emblem of a green wreath, in with a yellow crossed hammer and hoe (a local variation of the sickle), above which was placed a single yellow star. When, in 1991, multiparty democracy was restored, however, the original flag was re-adopted.

Note The Republic of the Congo *is often referred to as Congo-Brazzaville in order to differentiate it from the* Democratic Republic of the Congo, *known as Congo-Kinshasa (formerly Zaïre). See page 66.*

CONGO (CONGO-KINSHASA)

Formal name:
République Démocratic du Congo
(Democratic Republic of the
Congo)

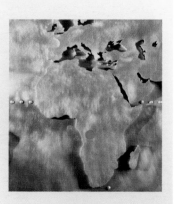

Formerly known as Zaïre (from *Zadi,* meaning "Big Water"), the name given to the region by the Portuguese explorers during the 15th century, the country was not fully explored by Europeans until Dr. David Livingstone and Henry Morton Stanley arrived during the 1870s, their expeditions being partly financed by the Belgian king, Leopold II, who established the Congo Free State in 1885. Having become a colony of the Belgian Congo in 1908, it achieved independence as the Republic of the Congo in 1960.

Since 1960, Congo-Kinshasa has had three different flags: the first (1960–63), the same as the current flag, was based on an earlier colonial flag featuring a blue field and single gold star, to which six additional stars, representing the provinces, were added down the hoist. The second flag (1963–71) had a blue field with single yellow star in the canton and a diagonal, red stripe fimbriated with yellow. The country, which was renamed the Democratic Republic of the Congo in 1964, was torn by civil war during the 1960s before being reunited in 1971 as Zaire, when a third flag, in Pan-African colors featuring the emblem of a hand holding a flaming torch, was introduced. When the government was overthrown in 1997, the country's flag and name at the time of independence were restored.

Note *The Democratic Republic of the Congo is often referred to as Congo-Kinshasa to differentiate it from the Republic of the Congo (known as Congo-Brazzaville).* See page 65.

Capital city:
Kinshasa

Location:
Central Africa

Currency:
1 zaïre = 100 makuta

Languages:
French, Swahili, diverse tribal
languages

Religions:
Christian, Animist

Flag adopted:
May 17, 1997

Flag ratio:
2:3

Formal name:
República de Costa Rica
(Republic of Costa Rica)

Capital city:
San José

Location:
Central America

Currency:
1 colón = 100 céntimos

Language:
Spanish

Religion:
Roman Catholic

Flag adopted:
October 21, 1964

Flag ratio
3:5

Originally inhabited by the Guaymi people, Costa Rica was visited by Christopher Columbus in 1502, colonized by Spanish settlers during the late 16th century, and remained under Spanish rule until 1821, when it gained its independence.

Part of the United Provinces of Central America (with El Salvador, Guatemala, Honduras, and Nicaragua) from 1824, Costa Rica declared itself an independent republic in 1834, but retained the flag of the United Provinces: three horizontal bands in the order blue-white-blue, with a central emblem of the federation. In response to revolutionary events taking place in France, in 1848 it was decided to incorporate the colors of the *Tricolore* into a new Costa Rican flag, a central, red stripe being inserted. The national seal was also created in 1847, and this was added to the flag in 1906. The arms depict two merchant ships sailing on two seas – the Pacific Ocean (foreground) and Caribbean Sea (background) – separated by three volcanoes representing Costa Rica's three main mountain ranges. Behind is a rising sun and seven stars, one for each of the provinces. (In 1906 there were only five provinces and therefore five stars, two stars being added in 1964 to represent two newly incorporated provinces.) Above is the country's name and a blue ribbon bearing the words "America Central," recalling the United Provinces.

COTE D'IVOIRE

The region now known as *Côte d'Ivoire* (Ivory Coast in English) was once made up of numerous kingdoms. During the 16th century, the British, French, and Portuguese established trading centers along the coast of the Gulf of Guinea to deal in slaves and the ivory that gave the country its name. Côte d'Ivoire became a French colony during the nineteenth century and part of French West Africa in 1904. Self-government was gained in 1958, and full independence achieved in 1960.

As with many other former French colonies, Côte d'Ivoire's flag is modeled on the French *Tricolore,* although it was also influenced by the Pan-African colors that Ghana first used in its flag. (The Côte d'Ivoire flag was adopted in 1959, just before independence, at a time when an alliance was being proposed with Niger, Chad, and Dahomey (modern Benin), causing each country to select a flag to denote their common interests. Although the alliance did not develop as planned, the flags were retained.) The three vertical stripes of the flag represent the savannahs of the northern lands (orange), the country's rivers and national unity (white), and the agriculture of the southern region (green).

Formal name:
République du Côte d'Ivoire
(Republic of Côte
d'Ivoire/Ivory Coast)

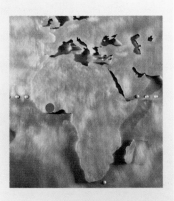

Capital cities:
Yamoussoukro (political),
Abidjan (economic)

Location:
West Africa

Currency:
1 C.F.A. franc = 100 centimes

Languages:
French, diverse tribal languages

Religions:
Muslim, Christian, diverse local
religions

Flag adopted:
December 3, 1959

Flag ratio:
2:3

Formal name:
Republika Hrvatska
(Republic of Croatia)

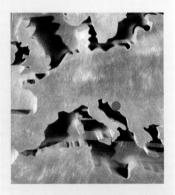

Capital city:
Zagreb

Location:
Central Europe

Currency:
1 kuna = 100 lipa

Languages:
Croatian, Serbian

Religions:
Roman Catholic, Serbian
Orthodox, Muslim

Flag adopted:
December 21, 1990

Flag ratio:
1:2

For some eight-hundred years following 1102, Croatia was an autonomous kingdom under the Hungarian crown, although it was often a battleground between Hungary, Byzantium, and Venice. In 1524, the country came under the rule of the Ottoman Empire, returning to the Hungarian crown in 1699. Alternating between Austrian and Hungarian rulership during the 19th century, in 1919 it was included in the kingdom of the Serbs, Croats, and Slovenes (which was named Yugoslavia in 1929). It declared itself independent in June 1991.

While it was part of Yugoslavia, Croatia's flag flew the Pan-Slavic colors of red, white, and blue. Following its invasion by Germany during World War II, a Nazi puppet state called Greater Croatia was formed, arms being added to the center of the national flag. Following Croatia's postwar reintegration into Yugoslavia, the tricolor was retained, and a red, gold-fimbriated star representing socialism was placed in the center. The flag in current use is based on the one that was used during World War II and depicts a red-white checkered shield (the traditional emblem of Croatia), above which are smaller shields representing, from left to right, the ancient arms of Croatia, Dubrovnik, Dalmatia, Istria, and Slavonia.

CUBA

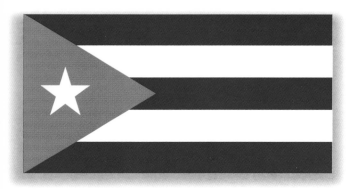

In 1492, Christopher Columbus claimed Cuba and its islands for Spain, and from 1511 it was a Spanish colony whose economy was based on sugar plantations worked by slaves who were first transported to the island in 1523 to replace the decimated Arawak population. (Slavery was abolished only in 1886.) Although Cuba became independent of Spain in 1898, at the end of the Spanish–American War, it was instead ceded to the United States. Early enthusiasm for the new administrative power faded, a republic was declared in 1901, and independence achieved in 1902 (although the United States retained its naval base on the island and the right to intervene in internal politics until 1934).

Cuba's flag, colloquially known as *La Estrella Solitaria* ("The Lone Star"), which was designed in 1848 for the liberation movement led by Narciso Lopez, was based on the "revolutionary" flags of both the U.S. and France. The three blue stripes represent Cuba's three original provinces and the two white ones the purity of the nation's ideals. The red triangle of the hoist signifies the three concepts of liberty, equality, and fraternity, as well as the blood sacrificed by Cuban patriots. The lone white star on the red triangle at first signified Cuba's desire to become a U.S. state, but is now interpreted as indicating its status as an independent nation.

Formal name:
República de Cuba
(Republic of Cuba)

Capital city:
La Habana (Havana)

Location:
Caribbean

Currency:
1 Cuban peso = 100 centavos

Language: Spanish
Religion: Roman Catholic

Flag adopted:
May 20, 1902

Flag ratio:
1:2

CYPRUS

Formal name:
Kypriaki Dimokratia
(Greek)

Kibris Cumhuriyeti
(Turkish)

(Republic of Cyprus)

Capital city:
Levkosia (Nicosia)

Location:
Eastern Mediterranean

Currency:
1 Cyprus pound = 100 cents

Languages:
Greek, Turkish, English

Religions:
Greek Orthodox, Muslim

Flag adopted:
August 16, 1960

Flag ratio:
3:5

For centuries, the strategic position of Cyprus between Europe, the Middle East, and North Africa has made it a coveted island. Ruled by the Assyrians, Babylonians, Egyptians, and Persians before being seized by Rome in 58 B.C., from A.D. 359 it was part of the Byzantine Empire until claimed by the English during the Third Crusade in 1191. Annexed by Venice in 1489, the island became part of the Ottoman Empire in 1571 before returning to British administration in 1878. During the 1950s, while Greek Cypriots campaigned for *enosis* (union) with Greece, Turkish Cypriots advocated partition, and Cyprus became an independent republic in 1960, power being shared by the two communities. The compromise failed in 1963, however, and U.N. forces were detailed to police the island. Following a pro-*enosis* coup in 1974, Turkish troops invaded northern Cyprus, dividing the country along what became known as the "Attila Line" and forming a separate, unofficial state called the Turkish Republic of Northern Cyprus.

The Cypriot flag, a white field with a copper-colored silhouette of the island in the center, supported by green olive branches (symbols of peace), represents an attempt to devise a neutral flag, indicating harmony between the two communities.

Note
Though technically the flag of the entire island, it is used only by the Greek community south of the Attila Line.

THE CZECH REPUBLIC

Formal name:
Ceska Republika
(Czech Republic)

Following the breakup of the Austro-Hungarian Empire at the end of World War I, an independent republic called Czechoslovakia was created from Bohemia and Slovakia, its first flag being designed to express the unity of the new country. Bohemia's red-over-white flag was the basis for this Czechoslovakian flag, a blue triangle being added in the hoist to represent Slovakia, the three colors used furthermore being considered traditional Slavic colors. During the Nazi occupation of Czechoslovakia in World War II, the use of this flag was banned, a horizontal tricolor of white, red, and blue being flown instead until 1945, when the country was liberated and the original flag restored.

When, in 1992, the Czechs and Slovaks agreed to separate, under the terms of the so-called "Velvet Divorce," neither successor state was allowed to use the national symbols of the previous federation. Because the traditional Czech (i.e., Bohemian) flag of red over white was seen being as too similar to Poland's, the new Czech Republic therefore decided to retain the tricolored flag, in defiance of their previous agreement.

Capital city:
Praha (Prague)

Location:
Central Europe

Currency:
1 koruna = 100 halura

Languages:
Czech, Slovak, Polish

Religions:
Roman Catholic, Protestant

Flag adopted:
March 30, 1920

Flag ratio:
2:3

Formal name:
Kongeriget Danmark
(Kingdom of Denmark)

Capital city:
København (Copenhagen)

Location:
Northern Europe

Currency:
1 Danish krone = 100 øre

Language:
Danish

Religion:
Lutheran

Flag adopted:
1625

Flag ratio:
28:37

The original home of the Danes was, in fact, Sweden, from which the first settlers emigrated during the 5th and 6th centuries. Ruled by local chieftains, during the 8th and 9th centuries their descendants terrorized Northern Europe with their Viking raids before being unified and Christianized by Harald Bluetooth, king of Denmark. King Knut (Canute) later ruled an empire that encompassed Denmark, Norway, and England, but this declined following his death in 1035. Beset by territorial wars and dynastic disputes, King Valdemar IV finally restored order during the 1350s, Denmark, Norway, and Sweden being united under Queen Margrethe I in 1397. Sweden broke away in 1449, however, while Norway was ceded to Sweden in 1815.

The oldest monarchy in Europe (but a constitutional monarchy only since 1953), Denmark also boasts its oldest flag, the *Dannebrog* ("Danish Cloth"). Although legend says that a red flag bearing a white cross appeared in 1219 to Valdemar II as a sign from heaven during his conquest of Estonia, it is more likely that the flag was received as gift from the pope during the Crusades. The flag was originally square, the design subsequently being elongated to extend the arm of the cross in the fly. Because several other Scandinavian countries were at one time ruled by Denmark, many of their flags were based on the Danish model.

DJIBOUTI

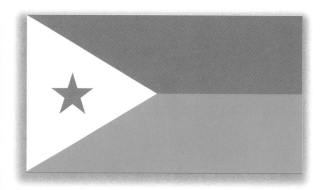

During the 9th century, Arabs brought Islam to the local Afars who inhabited the area now known as Djibouti, and from the 13th to the 17th centuries a series of wars was fought between the Afar Islamic states and Christian Ethiopia. In 1862, the French arrived to counter the British presence in Aden, near the southern entrance to the Red Sea, and the area was annexed and named French Somaliland in 1884. Renamed the French Territory of the Afars and Issas in 1967, opposition to French rule subsequently grew, the calls for independence becoming more frequent and occasionally violent. Independence as the Republic of Djibouti was finally achieved in 1977, whereupon the new government embarked on the task of uniting the Afars (who traditionally had strong links with Somalia) and the Issas (who had links with Ethiopia).

The flag adopted at independence was based on that of the *Ligue Populaire pour l'Independence* (People's League for Independence, L.P.A.), whose flag had a triangle-and-star arrangement, although for the new flag of Djibouti the star was placed in an upright position and the proportions altered to create a longer flag. The upper, light-blue band represents the Issa people, while the lower, green band symbolizes the Afars.

Formal name:
Jumhouriyya Djibouti
(Republic of Djibouti)

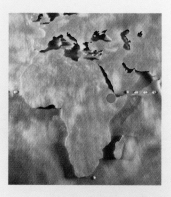

Capital city:
Djibouti City

Location:
East Africa

Currency:
1 Djibouti franc
= 100 centimes

Languages:
French, Arabic

Religion:
Muslim

Flag adopted:
June 27, 1977

Flag ratio:
4:7

Capital city:
Roseau

Location:
Caribbean

Currency:
1 East Caribbean dollar = 100 cents

Languages:
English (official language), French, Creole

Religion:
Roman Catholic

Flag adopted:
November 3, 1978

Flag ratio:
1:2

Sighted and named by Christopher Columbus on Sunday (*dies dominica* in Latin, hence the island's name), November 3, 1493, Dominica was inhabited first by the Arawak and then by the Carib peoples, who resisted all attempts at colonization until the French gained control of the island in 1632. Having passed to Britain in 1763, the island became part of the Leeward Islands' dependency in 1833 before joining the Windward Islands' group in 1940. In 1967, internal self-rule was achieved, full independence being awarded in 1978.

The flag adopted at independence features Dominica's national bird, the sisserou parrot (*Psittacus imperiala*), which is not only unique to the island, but also, regrettably, an endangered species. The bird stands on a twig encircled by ten yellow-fimbriated, green stars, representing the ten parishes of the country. This central emblem is superimposed on three horizontal and vertical stripes of yellow, black, and white, forming a triple-colored cross against the plain, green field. The cross represents religious faith, while the color yellow symbolizes sunshine, the island's citrus products, and the original Carib inhabitants; the white representing the island's clear rivers and waterfalls, as well as the purity of the nation's purpose; and the black denoting the island's rich soil and the African heritage of many of Dominica's people. Finally, the green of the field signifies the rich forests of the island.

DOMINICAN REPUBLIC

Formal name:
República Dominicana
(Dominican Republic)

The Dominican Republic occupies the eastern part of the island of Hispaniola, which it shares with Haiti. Discovered by Christopher Columbus in 1492, Hispaniola remained under Spanish control until 1795, when it was ceded to France. The eastern part of the island returned to Spanish rulership in 1809, but proclaimed its independence as the Dominican Republic in 1821. From 1822 to 1844, however, the Dominican Republic was annexed by Haiti.

The flag adopted in 1844 recalls the struggle for the republic's freedom from Haiti, a white cross of liberty, used by the independence movement, being superimposed on the blue and red of Haiti's flag (although the colors in the fly were transposed). The red is now interpreted as symbolizing the blood shed during the fight for independence, the blue signifies liberty, while the white cross represents the people's sacrifices. The state flag used by the government of the Dominican Republic includes the national coat of arms in the center of the cross. The arms depict a Bible, a gold cross, four flags, and two spears. Around the shield are olive and palm branches and above is the motto *Dios, Patria, Libertad* ("God, Country, and Liberty"). Below the shield are the words *República Dominicana* ("Dominican Republic").

Capital:
Santo Domingo

Location:
Caribbean

Currency:
1 Dominican peso
= 100 centavos

Language:
Spanish

Religion:
Roman Catholic, Protestant,
Spiritist

Flag adopted:
November 6, 1844

Flag ratio:
5:8

Formal name:
Timor Loro-Sae

DISPUTED FLAG

Capital city:
Dili

Location:
Southeast Asia

Currency:
Indonesian Rupiah

Languages:
Tetun, Javanese, Portuguese, Creole

Religions:
Roman Catholic, Animist

East Timor, on the island of Timor in the Malay Archipelago, was a former Portuguese colony. When the Portuguese withdrew in 1975, the Revolutionary Front of East Timor (F.R.E.T.I.L.I.N.) occupied Dili and proclaimed East Timor's independence, prompting neighboring Indonesia to invade East Timor, declaring it a province. This claim isn't recognized by the United Nations, however, and East Timor is currently under a United Nations' mandate.

For that reason, there is no special flag for this island, which technically still is part of Indonesia. The flag used in East Timor officially is the one of the United Nations. In 1975, East Timor was "independent" for a couple of days and flew the flag of the independence movement, but it would be wrong to publish that flag as the flag of East Timor. The island was then annexed by Indonesia. It is expected that East Timor will obtain independence in 2002 or 2003, when the country will also adopt its national flag.

ECUADOR

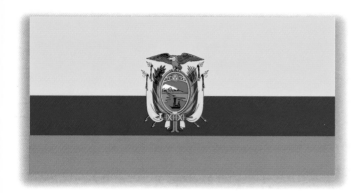

Formal name:
República del Ecuador
(Republic of Ecuador)

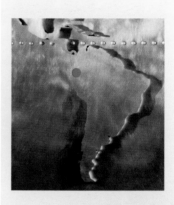

During the 15th century, most of Ecuador (the Spanish word for "equator") was part of the great Inca Empire. After the region was conquered by the Spanish (between 1532 and 1533), Ecuador was ruled as part of the viceroyalty of Peru. Liberated by the armies of Antonio José de Sucre and Simón Bolívar in 1822, it was initially federated with Colombia and Venezuela as the state of Gran Colombia, but in 1830 became completely independent.

The civil flags of Ecuador and Colombia are very similar: having both retained essentially the same flag of the confederation of Gran Colombia, each uses a horizontally arranged tricolor of yellow, blue, and red. Ecuador's civil flag is, however, of different proportions, and, when used abroad as the state flag, it always contains the country's coat of arms. This dates from 1845 and depicts an Andean condor atop an oval shield in which is depicted an allegorical scene of Mount Chimborazo (the continent's highest peak) and a ship at the mouth of the Guyas River (symbolizing trade), above which are the zodiacal signs for the months of March through May. The shield is surrounded by flags in the national colors supported on a *fasces* (a bundle of rods containing an ax), which signifies republicanism.

Capital city:
Quito

Location:
South America

Currency:
1 U.S. Dollar = 100 centaros

Languages:
Spanish, Quechua

Religion:
Roman Catholic

Flag adopted:
September 26, 1860

Flag ratio:
1:2

Formal name:
Jumhuriyat Misr al-'Arabiyah
(Arab Republic of Egypt)

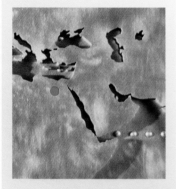

Capital city:
Al Qahirah (Cairo)

Location:
North Africa

Currency:
1 Egyptian pound
= 100 piastres

Language:
Arabic

Religions:
Sunni Muslim, Coptic Christian

Flag adopted:
October 4, 1984

Flag ratio:
2:3

Egypt's recorded history dates back to around 3100 B.C. It remained a kingdom – albeit ruled by successive dynasties throughout its long history – until 1953. The first national flag of modern Egypt was established by royal decree in 1923, when the country gained nominal independence from Britain. The flag consisted of a green field, with a white crescent and three stars in the middle.

King Farouk was overthrown in a coup in 1952, a republic being declared in the following year. In 1958, Egypt and Syria united to form the United Arab Republic (U.A.R.), whereupon the flag of the "Liberation Rally" which had led the 1952–53 revolt was adopted. The U.A.R. flag was a tricolor of red, white, and black bands, with two green stars in the middle of the central white stripe. In 1972, when the Federation of Arab Republics was formed, Egypt amended the flag, removing the stars and replacing them with the golden hawk of the Quraish (the emblem of the tribe of the Prophet Muhammad). This hawk was in turn removed in 1984, when it was replaced by an eagle (the symbol of Saladin, the sultan who ruled Egypt and Syria during the 12th century) bearing a shield with Egypt's national colors on its breast.

EL SALVADOR

Formal name:
República de El Salvador
(Republic of El Salvador)

From A.D. 100 until 1000, El Salvador was part of the Mayan kingdom that built the huge pyramids in the west of the country. Pipil Indians dominated the area until the Spanish conquered it in 1525, Spain subsequently governing it as part of Guatemala until 1821, when El Salvador was liberated. Having joined the United Provinces of Central America in 1823, although it seceded from the federation in 1838, El Salvador continued to use the federation's flag until 1865. It then adopted a national flag loosely based on the "Stars and Stripes."

El Salvador's current flag, which it adopted in 1912, is derived from the original United Provinces' flag, but with the arms of El Salvador in the center. The arms are based on a triangle (symbolizing equality) and depict five volcanoes (representing the five provinces), a cap of liberty, and the date of liberation. Surrounding this triangle are the five blue and white flags of the United Provinces within a wreath. The motto of Central America, *Dios, Union, Libertad* ("God, Union, Liberty") appears beneath. The whole is surrounded by the title of the state when it was part of the United Provinces.

Note *El Salvador uses different variants of the flag for civil, government, and military use. A blue and white flag without the coat of arms is the civil flag. With the arms, it is the state flag. A third version, with blue and white stripes and the motto* Dios Union, Libertad *written in yellow across the white stripe, is the governmental flag.*

Capital city:
San Salvador

Location:
Central America

Currency:
1 colón = 100 centavos

Languages:
Spanish

Religion:
Roman Catholic

Flag adopted:
May 17, 1912

Flag ratio:
3:5

EQUATORIAL GUINEA

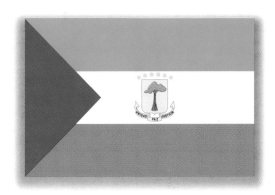

Formal name:
República de Guinea Ecuatorial
(Republic of Equatorial Guinea)

Capital city:
Malabo

Location:
West Africa

Currency:
1 C.F.A. franc = 100 centimes

Languages:
Spanish (official language),
English, Fang, Bubi

Religion:
Roman Catholic

Flag adopted:
October 12, 1968

Flag ratio:
2:3

The island of Bioko (formerly Macias Nguema Biyogo and previously Fernando Póo) was reached by Portuguese explorers in 1472, but was acquired by the Spanish in 1778, along with the coastal islands of Corisco, Elobey Grande, Elobey Chico, and Annobón (formerly Pagalu). The mainland section of Mbini (formerly Río Muni) was added in 1865, the whole area being Spanish Guinea. The country gained self-rule in 1963, full independence being achieved in 1968.

The national flag was flown on the first day of independence: a tricolor of green, white, and red horizontal bands, respectively symbolizing agriculture, peace, and independence. The blue triangle in the hoist signifies the sea that divides – and, at the same time, links – the African mainland to the five islands. Although the flag has contained a national emblem in its center since 1968, from 1972 to 1975, the period of the dictatorship of Francisco Ngeuma, the arms contained different tools, war flags, and swords, as well as the motto *Trabajo* ("work"). When Ngeuma was deposed, the original arms were restored. They consist of a silver shield charged with a silk-cotton tree, above which are six yellow, six-pointed stars (representing the mainland and the five islands), while beneath the shield is the national motto: *Unidad-Paz-Justicia* ("Unity-Peace-Justice").

ERITREA

During the 10th century, Eritrea was part of neighboring Ethiopia, falling to the Ottoman Empire during the mid-16th century and becoming an Italian colony in 1890. From 1941 to 1952 it was under British administration before becoming an autonomous province of Ethiopia in 1962. Various secessionist movements sprang up thereafter, heralding a civil war which began in 1971 and ended in 1991, when the collapse of the Ethiopia's communist government led to the recognition of Eritrea's right to independence.

During the 1950s, when it was a province of Ethiopia, Eritrea flew its own flag, which consisted of a light-blue field, with a green olive wreath and central branch in the middle. This continued to be flown as a "flag of liberation" until independence was finally achieved in 1993. The Eritrean People's Liberation Front (E.P.L.F.), which had campaigned for independence, had used a flag that was green over blue, with a red triangle in the hoist containing a gold star. At independence, although the new national flag retained the colors and pattern of the E.P.L.F. flag, the olive-wreath-and-branch emblem of the provincial flag (altered from green to gold) were added to the hoist.

Formal name:
State of Eritrea

Capital city:
Asmara

Location:
Northeast Africa

Currency:
1 nafka = 100 cents

Languages:
English, Arabic, Tigrinya

Religions:
Coptic Christian, Muslim

Flag adopted:
May 24, 1993

Flag ratio:
2:3

Formal name:
Eesti Vabariik
(Republic of Estonia)

Capital city:
Tallinn

Location:
Northeast Europe

Currency:
I kroon = 100 senti

Languages:
Estonian, Russian

Religions:
Lutheran, Russian Orthodox

Flag adopted:
May 8, 1990

Flag ratio:
7:11

Estonia was ruled by Denmark (1227–1346), German Teutonic Knights (1346–1558), and Sweden (1558-1712) before becoming part of the Russian Empire during the 19th century. The tricolor flag of Estonia was first used in 1881, during student uprisings against the czarist Russian occupation. Following the Russian Revolution in 1917, Estonia enjoyed a brief period of independence, during which its blue, black, and white flag was flown. The victorious Soviet forces of 1917 were, however, vanquished when Germany invaded Estonia during World War I. Although Soviet rule was re-established in November 1918, it was again overthrown in 1919, when Estonia declared itself independent and established a democratic republic. A fascist coup having taken place in 1934, however, in 1939 a secret deal between Germany and the Soviet Union resulted in Estonia becoming part of the U.S.S.R. The national tricolor having been outlawed by Stalinist forces, Estonia's national flag was not flown again until 1990, when the U.S.S.R. was dissolved.

The colors of the flag are representative of Estonia's history: blue is the color of loyalty, as well as representing the country's lakes and sky; black symbolizes the country's past sufferings and is both the color of the Estonian soil and the traditional peasant's jacket; while white represents the snow, birch bark, and Estonia's struggle for freedom.

ETHIOPIA

Formal name:
Ityo'pia
("Ethiopia," officially: Federal
Democratic Republic of
Ethiopia)

The oldest independent nation in Africa, which resisted colonization by European powers, Abyssinia (as Ethiopia was known until the 20th century) was the home of a powerful Christian kingdom that had been established during the 1st century A.D. In 1889, the by now fragmented kingdom was reunified by King Menelik II, who successfully countered an Italian invasion.

The three traditional national colors of green, yellow, and red that appear on the Ethiopian flag date back to the reign of Menelik II (1889–1913) and were first flown as three separate pennants in 1895. In Coptic Christianity, these colors individually symbolize faith, hope, and charity, and, when combined, the Holy Trinity. The three colors, along with black, became popular during the 1920s with the African-American activist Marcus Garvey, who sought a new homeland for black Americans in Africa, his activists in Jamaica looking to Emperor Haile Selassie (1892–1975) – also known as *Ras Tafari*, the "Lion of Judah" – for spiritual and political leadership during the 1930s. The emperor was deposed in 1974, however, and Ethiopia was declared a socialist state. The regime having been in turn overthrown in 1991, in 1994 a new constitution established Ethiopia as a federation, whereupon a central blue disk containing an emblem of a star and stylized sunrays, intended to signify both the diversity and unity of the country, was added.

Capital city:
Addis Abeba (Addis Ababa)

Location:
Northeast Africa

Currency:
I Ethiopian birr = 100 cents

Languages:
Amharic, Afaan Oromo, Tigrigna

Religions:
Ethiopian Orthodox, Muslim

Flag adopted:
February 6, 1996

Flag ratio:
1:2

FIJI

Formal name:
Matanitu Ko Viti
(Republic of the Fiji Islands)

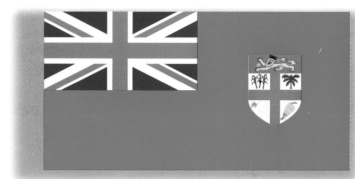

Capital city:
Suva

Location:
Pacific Ocean

Currency:
1 Fiji dollar = 100 cents

Languages:
English, Fijian, Hindustani

Religions:
Christian, Hindu

Flag adopted:
October 10, 1970

Flag ratio:
1:2

Fiji is made up of more than 800 islands and islets in the Pacific Ocean. Originally inhabited by Polynesian and Melanesian peoples, although Fiji's first European visitor was the Dutch explorer Abel Tasman in 1643, regular contact with Europe did not begin until the early 19th century. In 1874, Fiji became a British possession and remained a colony until independence.

Fiji's flag, which flew for the first time on Independence Day,(October 10, 1970) was the result of a competition won jointly by Mr. Robi Wilcock and Mrs. Murray MacKenzie. The country's continued political and economic ties with Britain are emphasized by the fact that Fiji's flag is based on the British Blue Ensign, but with a paler blue field. This symbolizes the Pacific Ocean and the vital role that it plays in Fiji's culture and economy. The flag also carries the British Union Jack in its canton (and continued to do so between 1987 and 1997, when Fiji left the Commonwealth). On the fly is Fiji's coat of arms, which was granted in 1980, a white shield with a red cross and red chief (upper third of the shield) bearing a British lion holding a coconut. Depicted in the quarters are a sugar-cane plant, a coconut palm, a dove of peace, and a bunch of bananas.

FINLAND

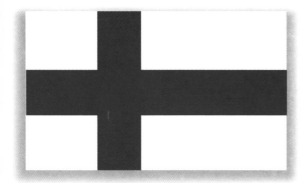

Formal name:
Suomen Tasavalta/Republiken Finland
(Republic of Finland)

Capital city:
Helsingfors (Helsinki)

Location:
Northern Europe

Currency:
1 markka = 100 penniä

Languages:
Finnish, Swedish

Religion:
Protestant

Flag adopted:
May 26, 1918

Flag ratio:
11:18

The nomadic Saami, or Lapps, were the earliest-known inhabitants of the region that is today called Finland, but from about the 1st century B.C. Finnic nomads from Asia gradually drove them into Saamiland, in the far north of Finland above the Arctic Circle. During the 12th century Finland was conquered and ruled by Sweden, for the next 200 years serving as the battleground for wars between Sweden and Russia. In 1809, during the Napoleonic Wars, Finland passed into Russian control, becoming a grand duchy ruled by the Russian czar. Nationalist feeling grew, however, and Finland proclaimed its independence during the 1917 Russian Revolution. Having initially tried to re-establish control over the country, in 1920 the Soviet regime acknowledged Finland's independence.

Although it was adopted as the national flag in 1918, the design of the Finnish flag dates from the 19th century. Like other flags from this region, Finland uses a "Scandinavian cross," in which the upright arm is set closer to the hoist than the fly. The blue of the cross represents Finland's lakes – of which there are some 60,000 – while the white field represents the snow that covers the land for four to five months a year in the south of the country, and for about seven months in the north.

Formal name:
République Française
(French Republic)

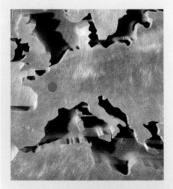

Capital city:
Paris

Location:
Western Europe

Currency: euro
1 French franc = 100 centimes

Languages:
French

Religions:
Roman Catholic, Protestant,
Muslim

Flag adopted:
pluvoise 27, year II (February
15, 1794)

Flag ratio:
2:3

France remained a monarchy from A.D. 987, when Hugh was crowned the first king of the House of Capet, until 1792, when a republic was created during the French Revolution (1789–99). The Bourbon monarchy, restored in 1814, was subsequently replaced by the Second Republic in 1848, the empire in turn being restored under Napoleon III between 1852 and 1870, when France's defeat in the Franco–Prussian War prompted the establishment of the Third Republic.

Following the adoption of the famous red, white, and blue *Tricolore* as the national emblem of France in 1794, both its design and colors have been used by revolutionary movements and nascent nations across the world to represent their ideals, the red, white, and blue colors having come to represent the three ideals of the French Revolutions (as well as later ones): liberty, equality, and fraternity. The red-white-blue combination is credited to the Marquis de Lafayette, who devised a similar, tricolored cockade to be worn by the revolutionaries. (Red and blue were the colors of Paris that were used on the day that the Bastille was stormed, while white was the color of monarchy.) Having been created in 1790, the colors of the French flag were reversed (red originally appeared on the hoist) and revised in 1794. Although the flag went out of use following Napoleon's defeat at the Battle of Waterloo, it was re-adopted – again by Lafayette – in 1830, and has remained France's flag ever since.

GABON

Formal name:
République Gabonaise
(Gabonese Republic)

Gabon was colonized by the Fang and Omiene peoples between the 16th and 18th centuries, its first European visitors being the Portuguese, who arrived during the late 15th century to develop a slave trade that would last for some 400 years. Gabon became part of the French Congo in 1889, and a province of French Equatorial Africa from 1908, before gaining full independence in 1960.

Gabon adopted its first flag in 1959, prior to independence. This was similar to the present green-yellow-blue, horizontally arranged tricolor, except that the central yellow stripe was narrower in width and the French *Tricolore* was contained in the canton. Unlike other former French colonies in this region (which use a 2:3 ratio for their flags), Gabon's colonial flag had a ratio of 3:4, which was maintained after independence. The flag's green, yellow, and blue colors – a combination of the Pan-African colors of unity and the French national colors – are said respectively to represent the country's natural resources, the equator (which runs through Gabon), and the sea.

Capital city:
Libreville

Location:
West Africa

Currency:
1 C.F.A. franc = 100 centimes

Languages:
French, Bantu

Religion:
Christian

Flag adopted:
August 9, 1960

Flag ratio:
3:4

Formal name:
Republic of the Gambia

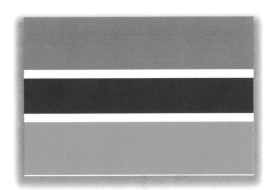

Capital city:
Banjul

Location:
West Africa

Currency:
1 dalasi = 100 butut

Languages:
English (official language),
Mandinka, Fulani, Wolof

Religions:
Muslim, Christian, Animist

Flag adopted:
February 18, 1965

Flag ratio:
2:3

Gambia, Africa's smallest country, was once part of the Muslim, gold-trading Mali Empire, which flourished in West Africa from the 7th to the 15th centuries until the Portuguese arrived in the region in 1455 and began slave-trading. During the late 16th century, the slave trade was taken over by the British, who established trading posts on the Gambia River. Having become a British colony in 1843, Gambia gained internal self-government in 1963, achieving full independence within the Commonwealth of Nations in 1965. A republic was declared in 1970, when an elected president replaced the British monarch as the official head of state.

Unlike many other African national flags, the horizontally striped flag adopted by Gambia at independence is not based on the colors of the leading political party, instead being said to represent the subtropical sun (red); the River Gambia – one of Africa's most navigable rivers – (blue) that flows through the country; and the dense mangrove, oil-palm, cedar, and mahogany forests (green) that grow along the river's banks.

GEORGIA

Formal name:
Sak'art'velos Respublika
(Republic of Georgia)

The Bagratid family established the Georgian kingdom during the 8th century, which gained in power until it ruled most of the Caucasian region. Following the Mongol invasions of the 13th century, from the 16th to the 18th centuries Georgia was disputed by the Persians and the Ottoman Turks. In 1762, an independent, united Georgia sought Russian protection, resulting in its annexation between 1801 and 1878. Following the Russian Revolution, a Georgian republic was established in 1918.

The Georgian flag, which originally had a ratio of 1:2, was the result of a competition won by Jakob Nikoladze in 1917. The flag's field was a deep red (Georgia's national color), while the black-and-white canton represented both Georgia's tragic past and its hopes for a better future. Georgia's independence lasted until 1921, when it became part of the Soviet Union, flying a version of the "Red Flag" that distinguished it from all of the other Soviet Socialist Republic's flags on account of the placement of the red hammer, sickle, and star on a blue disk in the canton, from which emanated 24 rays. In 1990, the year before the dissolution of the U.S.S.R., Georgia officially re-adopted its original national flag, altering its proportions to the current 3:5 ratio. The country was internationally recognized as an independent state on April 9, 1991.

Capital city:
Tbilisi

Location:
Southwest Asia

Currency:
lary

Languages:
Sakartvelo (Georgian),
Armenian, Russian

Religions:
Georgian Orthodox, Muslim,
Jewish

Flag adopted:
1918, re-adopted November
14, 1990

Flag ratio:
3:5

Formal name:
Bundesrepublik Deutschland
(Federal Republic of Germany)

Capital city:
Berlin

Location:
Western Europe

Currency:
euro, 1 deutschmark
= 100 pfennigs

Language:
German

Religion:
Lutheran (Protestant), Roman
Catholic

Flag adopted:
May 9, 1949

Flag ratio:
3:5

Germany did not become a unified nation until 1871. Before that time, it had been a confederacy (1815–67) and, prior to 1806, a federal empire composed of separate principalities. In 1949, the country was divided in two, to form the communist-led German Democratic Republic (G.D.R.), or East Germany, and the Federal Republic of Germany (F.R.G.), known as West Germany, the former German capital, Berlin, also being split by the Berlin Wall. The collapse of communist rule in East Germany in 1989, however, led to the reunification of the two states on October 3, 1990 as the Federal Republic of Germany.

The official name of the German flag is the *Bundesflagge* ("Federal Flag"), although most Germans call it the *Deutschlandfahne* ("German Flag"). The use of its black, red, and gold colors, which had been the colors of the uniforms of the German troops during the Napoleonic Wars, date from the time of the first attempts at unification in 1848. When the Weimar Republic was created in 1919, the horizontal tricolor that forms today's flag was re-adopted, but was replaced in 1933 by the *Hakenkreuz* (literally, the "Hooked Cross"), the Nazi Party's swastika flag. Although both East and West Germany reverted to the tricolor in 1949, the G.D.R. added its coat of arms to it. Since reunification, the German national flag has been the unadorned tricolor.

GHANA

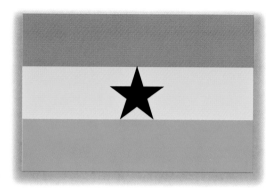

Formal name:
Republic of Ghana

The area now known as Ghana was once called the Gold Coast, and was made up of several powerful kingdoms, including those of the Fanti (on the coast) and the Ashanti (inland). The first Europeans arrived in 1471, the lucrative trade in gold, ivory, and slaves leading to the establishment of Portuguese, Dutch, Danish, Swedish, British, and French trading settlements in the region from about 1600. In alliance with the Fanti, the British eventually ousted their European competitors and established the colony of the Gold Coast in 1874, defeating the Ashantis in 1898. In 1917, the western part of Togoland (previously governed by Germany) also fell under British administration. Having taken the lead in becoming the first African colony to declare its independence in 1957, the Gold Coast changed its name to Ghana, after the great trading empire that had flourished in the region between the 5th and 13th centuries.

The flag that was adopted on independence was the first to use the Pan-African colors (red, yellow, green, and black, derived from the national colors of Ethiopia) that would inspire numerous new African national flags. The black star in the center of the flag, which is said to be the "Lone Star" of African freedom, was reputedly taken from Marcus Garvey's Black Star Line of 1919 to 1922, a shipping company intended to transport African-Americans from the United States to settle in Africa.

Capital city:
Accra

Location:
West Africa

Currency:
1 cedi = 100 pesewas

Languages:
English, numerous tribal languages

Religions:
Christian, Muslim, diverse traditional faiths

Flag adopted:
March 6, 1957

Flag ratio:
2:3

Formal name:
Elliniki Dhimokratia
(Hellenic Republic)

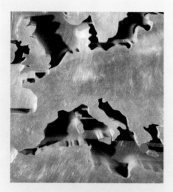

Capital city:
Athinai (Athens)

Location:
Southeast Europe

Currency:
1 drachma = 100 lepta

Language:
Greek

Religion:
Greek Orthodox

Flag adopted:
December 22, 1978

Flag ratio:
2:3

Although the history of Greece stretches back for many thousands of years, it did not become a modern state until 1822, during the War of Independence (1821–32), when it declared its independence from the Ottoman Empire, a monarchy being established under Prince Otto of Bavaria. Periods of internal conflict, civil unrest, and military coups have marked Greece's modern history, the monarchy being ousted in 1924, before being restored between 1935 and 1973. In 1974, however, a new constitution established the modern, multiparty, democratic Hellenic Republic.

The blue-and-white-striped flag, with a white cross on a blue field in the canton, has been in use since 1822. The nine stripes are said to represent the nine syllables of the Greek patriot's motto: *Eleutheria a Thanatos* ("Freedom or Death"), while the white cross symbolizes the Greek Orthodox religion. From 1832 to 1833, and also from 1975 to 1978, this flag was replaced (on land) by a simple, white cross on a blue field. The shade of blue has changed over the years, too, from the original light blue to the darker blue that was introduced during the 1970s. The proportions have also changed: originally 2:3, in 1970 a 7:12 ratio was adopted, the flag reverting to 2:3 in 1978, however.

GRENADA

Formal name:
State of Grenada

Although the tropical island of Grenada, the southernmost of the Windward Islands, was discovered by Christopher Columbus in 1498, the fierce resistance of the Carib people who inhabited the island prevented it from being colonized until 1650, when the French founded St. George's. Ceded to the British in 1783, Grenada remained a colony until 1958, when it became a member of the Federation of the West Indies until its dissolution in 1962. Internal self-government was achieved in 1967 and full independence in 1974.

The flag that was used by Grenada from 1967 to 1974 featured the island's major resource, a nutmeg, a motif that remained in the hoist of the flag that Grenada adopted on independence in 1974. In the red border surrounding the two yellow and two green triangles of today's flag stand six yellow, five-pointed stars, representing the six parishes of St. Andrew, St. David, St. John, St. Mark, St. Patrick, and the Grenadines. The seventh, central star, which is contained within a red disk, stands for the borough of St. George's, Grenada's capital. The colors, too, are symbolic: the red denotes courage and vitality, the green symbolizes agriculture and vegetation, and the yellow signifies wisdom and warmth.

Capital city:
St. George's

Location:
Caribbean

Currency:
1 East Caribbean dollar
= 100 cents

Language:
English, Creole

Religion:
Roman Catholic

Flag adopted:
February 7, 1974

Flag ratio:
3:5

Formal name:
República de Guatemala
(Republic of Guatemala)

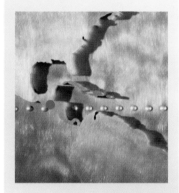

Capital city:
Guatemala City

Location:
Central America

Currency:
1 Guatemalan quetzal
= 100 centavos

Languages:
Spanish, Maya dialects

Religions:
Roman Catholic, Protestant

Flag adopted:
August 12, 1871

Flag ratio:
5:8

Guatemala was the center of the Maya civilization between the 4th and 9th centuries A.D., and despite having become the administrative center of Spanish Central America from 1524 until 1821, today the Maya continue to retain their distinct identity in the rural highlands of Guatemala. Having proclaimed its independence from Spain in 1821, Guatemala became part of the United Provinces of Central America from 1821 to 1839, flying the federation's flag until 1851.

Like other former members of the United Provinces, Guatemala's flag is still based on the federation's blue-and-white flag. Although a pro-Spanish faction seized power and added red and yellow to the flag in 1851, the original blue and white were restored in 1871, although the stripes were now arranged vertically rather than horizontally. In the center is the Guatemalan coat of arms, which was designed in 1871 by the Swiss artist Jean-Baptiste Frener (1821-97), who lived in Guatemala from 1856. The present form of the arms, which feature two golden rifles bound with laurel branches, was adopted in 1968. In the center is a parchment bearing the date of Guatemala's declaration of independence (*Libertad 15 de Septiembre de 1821,* "Liberated September 15, 1821"), above which is a quetzal bird, the country's symbol of independence.

GUINEA

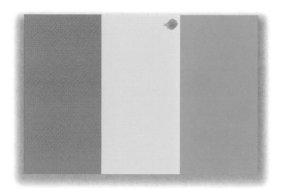

The Muslim Mali Empire ruled the region that is today known as Guinea between the 7th and 15th centuries. Portuguese explorers, followed by the British and French, established the slave trade there during the mid-15th century. France declared the eastern Boké region a protectorate in 1849, continuing to expand its territory until the colony of French Guinea was established in 1891. In 1958, Guinea voted for complete separation from France – unlike other former colonies, who became autonomous republics prior to independence – but suffered severe reprisals for having done so.

The French *Tricolore* nonetheless informed the design and proportions of Guinea's new flag, although the colors are those of the Pan-Africa Unity Movement. The symbolism of the flag's colors was also explained in a speech by Guinea's first president, Sékou Touré (1858–84), who said that red is the color of the blood of the freedom-fighters, as well the sweat of the workers; yellow is the color of both Guinean gold and the African sun, the source of light which shines on all people; while green is the color of the countryside. According to Touré, the three colors also reflect the words of Guinea's national motto: *Travail, Justice, Solidarité* ("Work, Justice, Solidarity").

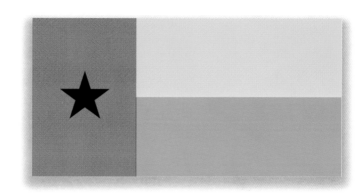

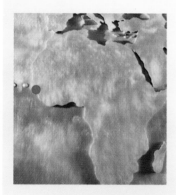

Capital city:
Bissau

Location:
West Africa

Currency:
1 C.F.A. franc = 100 centimes

Languages:
Portuguese, Crioulo (Creole)

Religions:
traditional beliefs dominate,
Muslim, Christian

Flag adopted:
September 24, 1973

Flag ratio:
1:2

The early history of Guinea-Bissau is largely unknown, but the country's major ethnic groups, the Balante, Fulani, Pepel, Malinke, and Mandyako peoples, were certainly well-established in the region by the 12th century. The first European to visit Guinea-Bissau was the Portuguese slave-trader Nuño Tristao, in 1446, and the area subsequently became a major center of the slave trade. Although a Portuguese post was established in Bissau in 1687, which was administered with the Cape Verde Islands from 1836, the colony of Portuguese Guinea was not created until 1879. National feeling began to be asserted during the 1950s, and after Portugal refused to grant the country its independence, Guinea-Bissau mounted a liberation war (1961–74), declaring itself independent in 1973.

The flag of Guinea-Bissau is based on one used by the *Partido Africano da Independencia da Guiné e Cabo-Verde* (African Party of Independent Guinea and Cape Verde, P.A.I.G.C.), which was based on the Pan-African colors and black star of African unity that was first used by Ghana in 1957 and also gave rise to Cape Verde's "old" flag. Although the P.A.I.G.C. continues to use its original flag, the national flag of Guinea-Bissau omits the party's initial letters below the star in the vertical red band.

GUYANA

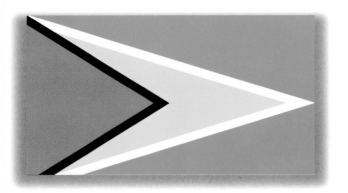

Formal name:
Cooperative Republic of
Guyana

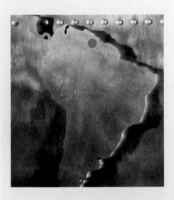

Although it is situated in the continent of South America, Guyana's history mirrors that of the smaller islands of the West Indies, in that it was not colonized by the Spanish or Portuguese, but by the Dutch in 1620. The colony was seized by the British in 1796, in 1831 being merged with Demerara, Berbice, and Essequibo to form British Guiana, whose capital was the former Dutch town of Stabroek, now renamed Georgetown. Following more than 150 years of colonial rule, British Guiana became independent in 1966, when it adopted the name Guyana, a Native American word meaning "Land of Waters."

The flag that Guyana adopted on gaining independence is known as the "Golden Arrowhead' after the arrowhead that flies across the green field. It was designed by Whitney Smith to reflect the country's physical nature, as well as the dynamism of its people. The golden arrowhead represents Guyana's mineral wealth; the red triangle signifies the dynamism of nation-building; while the black fimbriation denotes the endurance that will sustain the forward-thrusting Guyanese people. Finally, the color green represents the agriculture and forests of the land, and the white fimbriation denotes its rivers and spectacular waterfalls (Kaieteur Falls, on the Potaro River, is one of the highest single-drop waterfalls in the world).

Capital city:
Georgetown

Location:
South America

Currency:
1 Guyana dollar = 100 cents

Languages:
English, Hindi, Urdu, Creole,
Native American languages

Religions:
Hindu, Protestant, Roman
Catholic, Muslim

Flag adopted:
May 26, 1966

Flag ratio:
3:5

Formal name:
République d'Haïti/Republik Dayti
(Republic of Haiti)

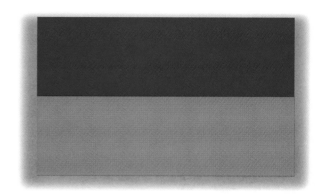

Capital city:
Port-au-Prince

Location:
Caribbean

Currency:
1 gourde = 100 centimes

Languages:
French, Creole

Religions:
Roman Catholic, Protestant

Flag adopted:
February 25, 1986

Flag ratio:
3:5

Haiti occupies the western portion of the island of Hispaniola (to the east is the Dominican Republic). Although the island was once a Spanish colony called Santo Domingo, the western (Haitian) part was colonized by France during the mid-17th century, formally becoming a French colony in 1697. Led by Toussaint L'Ouverture, in 1790 the black slaves who had been brought from Africa to work on the plantations revolted, took over the island, and abolished slavery. Slavery was, however, reinstated when L'Ouverture was killed by troops sent to re-establish France's control over the colony. Independence was eventually proclaimed in 1804, during a revolt led by Jean-Jacques Dessalines and Henri Christophe.

The first Haitian flag, which dates back to 1803, was made from the remnants of the French *Tricolore* that Dessalines reputedly tore apart. The blue and red sections were stitched together in a horizontal arrangement to represent the country's black and mulatto communities. From 1956 to 1986, Haiti was ruled by François Duvalier ("Papa Doc") and his son, Jean-Claude ("Baby Doc"), who kept control by means of their infamous army, the *Tontons Macoutes*. During this period, a second flag was used, consisting of vertically arranged black and red stripes. The original blue-and-red flag was reinstated at the end of the Duvaliers's regime.

Note *The Haitian national flag often varies in proportion and sometimes appears with a coat of arms within a white square in its center.*

HONDURAS

Formal name:
República de Honduras
(Republic of Honduras)

One of the largest Central American republics, Honduras was part of the Maya civilization (and a Maya pyramid is the central feature of the national coat of arms). Christopher Columbus reached the area in 1502, and from 1526 it was colonized by Spain. On September 15, 1821, Honduras gained its freedom from Spain to become part of the United Provinces of Central America (with Nicaragua, El Salvador, Guatemala, and Costa Rica) and adopted the federation's blue-and-white flag with a central, triangular emblem. The flag's blue bands were said to represent the Caribbean Sea and Pacific Ocean (apart from El Salvador, all of the states that belonged to the United Provinces are bordered by these seas). Honduras seceded from the United Provinces in 1839, however, declaring itself independent in the following year.

Like the other former members of the United Provinces, Honduras retained the blue-and-white, three-banded flag of the federation, although it altered the central emblem to five blue stars in 1866. These have been interpreted in different ways: as representing the original five states of the United Provinces, for example, or as expressing the hope that a similar Central American organization will be revived.

Capital city:
Tegucigalpa

Location:
Central America

Currency:
1 Honduran lempira
= 100 centavos

Languages:
Spanish, English, diverse Indian dialects

Religion:
Roman Catholic

Flag adopted:
February 16, 1866

Flag ratio:
1:2

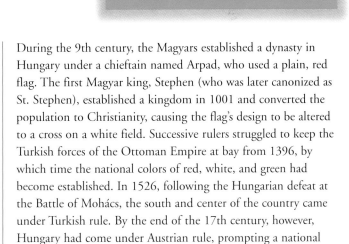

Formal name:
Magyar Köztársaság
(Republic of Hungary)

Capital city:
Budapest

Loction:
Central Europe

Currency:
1 forint = 100 filler

Language:
Magyar (Hungarian)

Religions:
Roman Catholic, Protestant

Flag adopted:
October 1, 1957

Flag ratio:
2:3

During the 9th century, the Magyars established a dynasty in Hungary under a chieftain named Arpad, who used a plain, red flag. The first Magyar king, Stephen (who was later canonized as St. Stephen), established a kingdom in 1001 and converted the population to Christianity, causing the flag's design to be altered to a cross on a white field. Successive rulers struggled to keep the Turkish forces of the Ottoman Empire at bay from 1396, by which time the national colors of red, white, and green had become established. In 1526, following the Hungarian defeat at the Battle of Mohács, the south and center of the country came under Turkish rule. By the end of the 17th century, however, Hungary had come under Austrian rule, prompting a national renaissance in 1815 under the leadership of Louis Kossuth.

Following the revolution of 1848 to 1849, a short-lived republic was declared (which remained part of the Austro-Hungarian Empire until 1918), whereupon today's horizontally banded tricolor of red, white, and green was adopted. A royal crown featured in the center of the flag until 1945, when the new republican regime replaced it with the "Kossuth" coat of arms until 1949. When Hungary fell under communist rule, the arms were replaced by a Soviet emblem. After the national uprising against the Stalinist government, and susbsequent Soviet invasion (1956), in 1957 Hungary adopted the plain tricolor as its national flag. Following the fall of the communist regime in 1990, the arms of the kingdom were restored, although they were not added to the national flag.

ICELAND

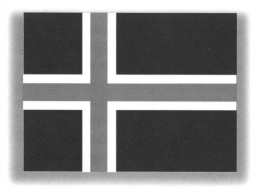

Formal name:
Lydveldid Ísland
(Republic of Iceland)

Iceland was first occupied in A.D. 874 by Vikings from Norway, who founded a republic and Europe's oldest parliament in A.D. 930. Having converted to Christianity in A.D. 1000, Iceland accepted Norwegian sovereignty in about 1263 in order to end a bitter civil war, and when Norway came under Danish rule in 1380, so, too, did Iceland, which continued to remain attached to Denmark even after Norway gained its independence in 1814. Icelandic nationalism grew during the 19th century, however, and although Iceland gained its independence in 1918, it remained linked to Denmark through their shared monarch, that is until 1944, when Iceland's citizens voted for complete independence in a referendum.

Iceland's first unofficial national flag was a white "Scandinavian cross" on a dark-blue field that was first flown in 1897. Modeled on the Danish flag, the current Icelandic flag was introduced in 1915 and officially adopted in 1918, when Iceland was a separate Danish realm and when the red of the Norwegian and Danish flags was added to the traditional blue-and-white colors of Iceland. The colors also symbolize Iceland's landscape: red for fire (Iceland has more than a hundred volcanoes), blue for water (denoting its spectacular geysers, lakes, and fast-flowing rivers), and white for ice (nearly 15 percent of the country's surface is covered by snowfields and glaciers).

Capital city:
Reykjavik

Location:
North Atlantic
Ocean/Northwestern Europe

Currency:
1 króna = 100 aurar

Language:
Icelandic

Religion:
Lutheran (Protestant)

Flag adopted:
June 19, 1915

Flag ratio:
18:25

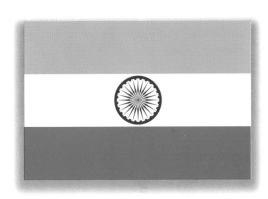

Formal name:
Bharatavarsha
(Republic of India)

Capital city:
New Delhi

Location:
Southern Asia

Currency:
1 Indian rupee = 100 paisa

Languages:
English, Hindi (at least 18 major languages and more than 1000 regional languages and dialects spoken)

Religions:
Hindu, Christian, Sikh, Muslim, Buddhist, Jain

Flag adopted:
July 22, 1947

Flag ratio:
2:3

India's long history stretches back to the Indus Valley civilization of about 2500 to 1700 B.C., and for many hundreds of years India was home to great empires and regional kingdoms, that is, until Britain began its conquest of the vast Indian subcontinent in 1757. British expansion was complete by 1858, and until 1947 India was the "British Raj," although following its foundation in 1885, the Indian National Congress (I.N.C.) became a focus for growing Indian nationalism. Along with independence in 1947 came the partition of India into a mainly Hindu India and predominantly Muslim Pakistan.

The flag adopted by India in 1947 was based on the I.N.C. flag, the colors of which symbolized Hinduism (orange), Islam (green), and the desire for unity and peace (white). The I.N.C. flag, which was hoisted as the "official" Indian flag in Berlin, Germany, in 1941, contained a blue spinning wheel in the center, an emblem that was derived from Mahatma Gandhi's call for economic self-sufficiency through spinning by hand. On independence, the spinning wheel was replaced with the Ashoka Chakra (the "Wheel of Law" of the 3rd-century Emperor Ashoka), in Buddhist belief the symbol of progress and change, whose 24 spokes correspond to the hours in a day.

INDONESIA

Formal name:
Republik Indonesia
(Republic of Indonesia)

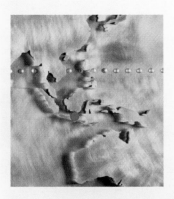

The powerful Buddhist kingdom of Srivijaya flourished on Sumatra between the 7th and 13th centuries A.D., but was eclipsed by the Java Hindu realm of Majapahit during the 13th to 15th centuries. By the 16th century, however, Islam, which had been introduced by Arab traders, had taken the place of both religions. At the same time, Dutch, English, and Portuguese traders were active in the area, and in 1595 Holland gained control of Indonesia, which became a Dutch colony administered by the Dutch East India Company in 1799. Indonesia gained its independence in 1949.

The flag of Indonesia is based on the Majapahit Empire's red-and-white, nine-striped banner. (The growing nationalism of the 1920s had led to a revival of the "holy" colors of red and white to symbolize opposition to Dutch rule, and the red-and-white flag was first flown in 1928.) The *Sang Saka* ("Lofty Bicolor") is the official name of the flag, although it is commonly called *Merah Putih* ("Red-White"). The red stripe symbolizes physical life, while the white stripe represents spiritual existence; together they stand for the complete human being – body and spirit. First adopted as the national flag when Indonesia proclaimed its independence in 1945, it continued to be used after the War of Independence (1945–49).

Capital city:
Jakarta

Location:
Southeast Asia

Currency:
1 Indonesian rupiah = 100 sen

Languages:
Bahasa Indonesian, Javanese, Sundanese, Dutch

Religions:
Christian, Sunni Muslim

Flag adopted:
August 17, 1945

Flag ratio:
2:3

Formal name:
Jomhuri-ye Eslami-ye Iran
(Islamic Republic of Iran)

Capital city:
Tehran

Location:
Southwest Asia

Currency:
1 touman
= 10 rials = 100 dinars

Languages:
Farsi (Persian), Turkic languages,
Kurdish

Religions:
Shi'ite Muslim, Christian

Flag adopted:
July 29, 1980

Flag ratio:
4:7

In 1979, the shah (king) of Iran – which the English-speaking world knew as "Persia" until 1935 – was overthrown following a revolution led by the Shi'ite cleric Ayatollah Khomeini, whereupon Iran was declared an Islamic republic.

Adopted in 1980, the national flag's colors of green (symbolizing Islam), white (peace), and red (courage) date from the 18th century and were arranged in horizontal stripes in the order green, white, and red, in 1907. Emblems of the Islamic Revolution replaced the original centerpiece of a lion and sword in 1980, the central symbol of four crescents and a sword representing the word *Allah* ("God"), and the five parts of the emblem symbolizing the five principles of Islam. Above the sword in the center is a *tashid* (which resembles a moustache or the letter "w"), which is used to double a letter in Arabic script, in this instance symbolically doubling the strength of the sword. The shape of the central emblem is also said to resemble a tulip (in ancient belief, red tulips being said to grow on the graves of patriots and martyrs). On the borderline of the stripes is the phrase *Allah Akbar* ("God is great"), which is written in stylized Kufic script and repeated 22 times, the number corresponding to the date in the Jallali Muslim calendar on which the Islamic Revolution of 1979 began.

Note *The hoist for the flag of Iran should be on the viewer's right because the flag features Arabic script, which is read from right to left.*

IRAQ

Formal name:
Al Jumhuriyah al'Iraqiyah
(Republic of Iraq)

Once part of the Ottoman Empire, Iraq became a monarchy under British mandate in 1920, before becoming fully independent in 1932. Its first flag of "independence" was used in 1920, and was a black, white, and green, horizontally striped tricolor, with a red trapezoid in the hoist and two seven-pointed stars.

A revolution deposed the royal family in 1958, and a second flag (with vertical stripes of black, white, and green, with a central yellow disk contained within an eight-pointed star), was adopted in the following year. This flag was used until 1963.

From 1963 to 1991 a third flag was used, consisting of a horizontally arranged, red, white, and black tricolor, with three green stars disposed along the white stripe. This was based on the Egyptian flag at that time, the three stars being included in Iraq's flag in anticipation of the political union of Iraq with Egypt and Syria, which, in the event, did not occur. Iraq's current flag is based on this version, the green *takbir* that spells out the words *Allah Akbar* ("God is great") in Arabic script having been added in January 1991, during the Gulf War. The flag's four Pan-Arabic colors symbolize the ideal qualities of Muslims, courage (red), generosity (white), and piety (green), as well as the triumphs of Islam (black).

Note *The hoist for the flag of Iraq should be on the viewer's right because the flag features Arabic script, which is read from right to left.*

Capital city:
Baghdad

Location:
Southwest Asia

Currency:
1 Iraqi dinar
= 20 dirhams = 1000 fils

Languages:
Arabic, Kurdish

Religion:
Muslim

Flag adopted:
first adopted July 31, 1963,
modified January 13, 1991

Flag ratio:
2:3

Formal name:
Poblacht na hÉireann
(Republic of Ireland), informally,
Eire

Capital city:
Baile Átha Cliath (Dublin)

Location:
Western Europe

Currency:
1 Irish pound = 100 pence

Languages:
Gaelic (Irish), English

Religions:
Roman Catholic, Protestant

Flag adopted:
constitutionally confirmed
December 29, 1937

Flag ratio:
1:2

Anglo-Norman adventurers first invaded Ireland in 1167, and by the end of the Middle Ages England had embarked on a policy of the conquest, confiscation, and plantation of Irish lands, a policy that led to the eventual subordination of Irish political and economic interests. The traditional flag of Ireland consisted of a green field bearing the golden-harp emblem of Brian Boru, Ireland's 11th-century king, and during the 19th century, when a movement for home rule was growing in strength, this "Green Flag" came to be seen as the symbol of an independent Ireland.

In 1848 – the year in which revolutions occurred throughout Europe – a green, white, and orange tricolor, whose design was influenced by the French *Tricolore*, was publicly unveiled in Waterford by Thomas Francis Meagher, a leader of the Young Ireland movement. During the Easter Rising of 1916, Irish nationalists seized Dublin's General Post Office, proclaimed a republic, and adopted this tricolor as their national flag. Following the establishment of the Irish Free State, in 1921, the tricolor was officially confirmed, being written into the constitution in 1937.

The flag's green stripe represents the Gaelic and Catholic communities, the orange stripe denotes Ireland's Protestants (originally supporters of William of Orange), while the white stripe symbolizes peace and the union of the two faiths.

ISRAEL

Formal name:
Medinat Yisrael
(State of Israel)

The Jewish national liberation movement known as Zionism, dedicated to the creation of a national homeland for the Jews, was founded during the 1890s. Palestine, the birthplace of Judaism and site of the ancient kingdom of Israel, became the focus for Jewish immigrants during the early 20th century. In 1947, following the United Nations' Resolution 147 on Palestine, the state of Israel was indeed created in Palestine.

The Israeli national flag predates the state by some fifty years, however, having been designed for the Zionist movement by David Wolfsohn in 1891. The flag bears the *Magen David* ("Shield of David"), a six-pointed star made up of two triangles, which, according to tradition, appeared on the shield of King David, slayer of the giant Goliath and father of King Solomon (who also used the emblem on his ring, hence its alternative name, "Solomon's Seal"). Having first been used as an official Jewish symbol in Prague (in the Czech Republic) in 1354, when the Jewish community was given the right to fly its own flag, the *Magen David* was subsequently used as a symbol of Judaism all over the world. The blue-and-white colors of the Israeli flag are said to have been derived from the *tallit*, the Jewish prayer shawl.

Capital city:
Yerushalayim (Jerusalem)

Location:
Southwest Asia

Currency:
1 new sheqel = 100 agorot

Languages:
Hebrew, Arabic

Religions:
Jewish, Muslim

Flag adopted:
November 12, 1948

Flag ratio:
8:11

Formal name:
Repubblica Italiana
(Italian Republic)

Capital city:
Roma (Rome)

Location:
Southern Europe

Currency:
1 lira = 100 centesimi

Languages:
Italian, diverse regional variants
(e.g.. Neapolitan, Sicilian,
Sardinian)

Religion:
Roman Catholic

Flag adopted:
June 19, 1946

Flag ratio:
2:3

Between 1796 and 1814, the collection of city-states, dukedoms, and monarchies that constituted Italy at that time were briefly united under French rule and introduced to the principles of the French Revolution. After Napoleon's fall, however, Italy was once again divided (between Austria, the papacy, and the kingdoms of Sardinia and Naples, as well as four smaller duchies). Despite the country's partition, nationalist ideals remained alive in Italy, the *Risorgimento* ("Resurgence") movement gathering pace from 1830 to culminate in the campaigns of Count Cavour and Giuseppe Garibaldi and finally, in 1861, in a united kingdom of Italy (following a referendum, in 1946 the monarchy was abolished and Italy became a republic).

The Italian tricolor is derived from the standard used by Napoleon during his Italian campaign of 1796, the design being based on the French *Tricolore,* and the green and white colors echoing the uniform of the Civic Militia of Milan. (Red was added when it became the National Guard in 1796, green, white, and red subsequently becoming the national colors of Italy.) The colors of the first tricolor were displayed horizontally from 1796 to 1798, when their disposition was changed to the current, vertical arrangement. In 1861, the year of the kingdom of Italy's birth, the tricolor carried the arms of the House of Savoy, of which the new king, Victor Emmanuel I, was a scion. These were removed when a republic was proclaimed in 1946, however, thereby creating the current flag.

JAMAICA

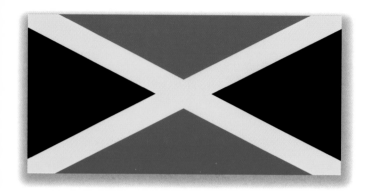

Originally inhabited by the Arawak people, the island of Jamaica was sighted by Christopher Columbus in 1494, who claimed it for Spain, the Spanish governing the island until 1655, when it became a British colony. Granted internal self-government in 1958, Jamaica joined the West Indies Federation before gaining full independence in 1962.

The Jamaican flag is the result of a national competition, and although a saltire (a diagonal cross stretching from corner to corner) forms the basis of the design, this does not have any religious significance. The golden arms of the cross divide the flag into four triangles: two green ones at the top and bottom and two black ones at the fly and hoist. As well as being Pan-African colors that recall the African origins of many Jamaicans, the gold, green, and black also respectively symbolize the Caribbean sunshine and Jamaica's rich, natural resources; its agricultural wealth (it boasts more than two-hundred species of flowering plants, as well as indigenous and cultivated trees) and hopes for the future; as well as the hardships borne by its people. Together, the colors represent the Jamaican motto "Burdens and hardships there may be, but we have hope and the sun still shines."

Formal name:
Jamaica

Capital city:
Kingston

Location:
Caribbean

Currency:
1 Jamaican dollar = 100 cents

Language:
English

Religions:
Protestant, Roman Catholic, Rastafarian

Flag adopted:
August 6, 1962

Flag ratio:
1:2

Formal name:
Nihon Koku, informally, Nihon or Nippon
(Japan)

Capital:
Tokyo

Location:
Eastern Asia

Currency:
1 yen = 100 sen

Languages:
Japanese, Korean, Chinese

Religions:
Shinto, Buddhist, Christian

Flag adopted:
January 27, 1870

Flag ratio:
2:3

From the 12th to the mid-19th century, shoguns (military rulers) shared power with the emperor, who had ruled Japan since the 7th century. First contact with Europeans occurred in 1542, when Portuguese traders arrived, soon followed by the Spanish and Dutch. Although Christianity was introduced to Japan by Francis Xavier in 1549, fearing that religious conversion was a precursor to invasion, Japan subsequently expelled most foreigners and introduced the policy of *sakoku*, self-imposed isolation from the rest of the world. This state of affairs lasted until 1853, when trade relations with the United States commenced.

The Japanese flag dates from 1870, when power was removed from the shoguns and restored to the Meiji Emperor. Officially called the *Hi-no-maru* ("Sun Disk"), it is both the state *Mon* (emblem) and the visual expression of Japan's name, *Nihon* meaning "Origin of the Sun." Legend states that the sun was the ancestor of the Japanese emperors, and the *Hi-no-maru* has been used as an imperial badge since the 14th century. The current flag differs slightly from the original flag of 1870, which had an overall proportion of 7:10, with the red disk being positioned fractionally toward the hoist, new legislation of 1999 setting the flag at a ratio of 2:3 and positioning the disk centrally.

JORDAN

Formal name:
Al-Mamlaqa al-Urduniyya al-Hashimiyya
(Hashemite Kingdom of Jordan)

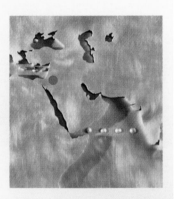

Capital:
Amman

Location:
Southwest Asia

Currency:
1 Jordanian dinar = 1000 fils

Language:
Arabic

Religion:
Sunni Muslim

Flag adopted:
April 16, 1928

Flag ratio:
1:2

Once part of the Byzantine Empire, during the 16th century Jordan passed to the Ottoman Empire, until the latter was dissolved following World War I. Then known as Transjordan, in 1920 the League of Nations gave the mandate to administer the area east of the River Jordan to Britain. In 1923, Transjordan became a separate emirate, achieving full independence as the kingdom of Jordan under Amir Abdullah (1880–1951) in 1946.

The design of the Jordanian flag is derived from the Arab Revolt flag used by Syria, Iraq, and Jordan in 1917 during their fight against Ottoman rule, the order of the stripes on this flag having been established as black-white-green in 1920. The colors are those adopted by the Pan-Arabic nationalist movement, the black, white, and green bands respectively symbolizing the Arab Abbasid, Umayyad, and Fatimid dynasties, while the red triangle in the hoist that unites the bands represents the rule of the Hashemite kings (the Jordanian king being the only surviving ruler of this dynasty) and their descent from the Prophet Muhammad. In 1928, after Jordan had gained nominal independence as an emirate, the seven-pointed Islamic star was added to the flag, the seven points standing for the *Fatiha*, the first seven *surahs* (verses) of the Qur'an.

KAZAKHSTAN

Formal name:
Qazaqstan Respublikasy
(Republic of Kazakhstan)

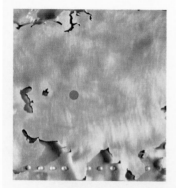

Capital city:
Astana

Location:
Central Asia

Currency:
1 tenge = 100 tyin

Languages:
Kazakh, Russian

Religion:
Sunni Muslim

Flag adopted:
June 4, 1992

Flag ratio:
1:2

Ruled by the Mongols from the 13th century, the region that is today known as Kazakhstan came under Russian control during the 18th century, prompting increasing resentment of czarist rule. Following a major Kazakh revolt during World War I, in 1917, after the Bolshevik Revolution, Kazakh nationalists formed a local government and demanded autonomy. The Soviet response was to order the Red Army to invade the region in 1920, whereupon the Kirghiz Autonomous Soviet Socialist Republic (A.S.S.R.) was established (which should not be confused with the Kara-Kirghiz A.S.S.R., now Kyrgyzstan), the name being changed to the Kazakh A.S.S.R. in 1926. Having become a full union republic within the U.S.S.R. in 1936, in September 1991 Kazakhstan declared itself independent, in December 1991, upon the dissolution of the U.S.S.R., joining the Commonwealth of Independent States (C.I.S.).

Officially recognized as an independent republic since 1991, Kazakhstan's post-independence flag is light blue (similar in color to the earlier A.S.S.R. flag), symbolizing both the blue skies of the country and its hopes for the future. Depicted on the field is a stylized *berkut* (the native eagle of the Steppes) beneath a golden sun from which emanates 32 rays, which together symbolize the Kazakh people's freedom. On the hoist, also in gold, is an intricate, vertical pattern, which is officially described as the "national ornamentation."

KENYA

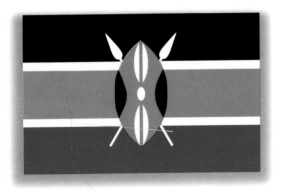

Formal name:
Jamhuri ya Kenya
(Republic of Kenya)

Archeological evidence shows that the area now known as Kenya was first inhabited some 5 million years ago by African tribal groups. Colonized by Arabs during the 8th century, the region came under Portuguese rule from the 15th to 18th centuries, but was forcibly appropriated by the British in 1895, when it became part of the East African Protectorate before becoming a British colony in 1920. Resentment against Britain grew, however, particularly following the seizure of Kikuyu tribal lands, and the protest movement of the 1920s eventually developed into a powerful nationalist movement spearheaded by the Kenya Africa National Union (K.A.N.U.) led by Jomo Kenyatta. Kenya finally became independent in 1963 and a republic in 1964, Kenyatta becoming the republic's first president.

The flag that Kenya adopted on attaining independence is based on the K.A.N.U. flag of horizontal bands in the order black-red-green (the colors respectively symbolizing the black majority, the blood that is common to all humans, and the fertility of the Kenyan lands), to which was added white fimbriation derived from the flag of the K.A.N.U.'s rival political party, the Kenya African Democratic Union Party, to signify peace and national unity. In the center of the flag is a traditional Masai warrior's shield and two spears, which together represent the defense of freedom.

Capital city:
Nairobi

Location:
East Africa

Currency:
1 Kenya shilling = 100 cents

Languages:
Swahili, English

Religions:
Protestant, Roman Catholic, Muslim, diverse others

Flag adopted:
December 12, 1963

Flag ratio:
2:3

KIRIBATI

Formal name:
Republic of Kiribati

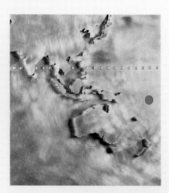

Capital city:
Tarawa

Location:
West-central Pacific Ocean

Currency:
1 Australian dollar = 100 cents

Languages:
Kiribati, English

Religions:
Protestant, Roman Catholic

Flag adopted:
July 12, 1979

Flag ratio:
1:2

Situated some 2,500 miles (about 4,000 kilometers) southwest of Hawaii, Kiribati consists of 33 coral islands (21 are inhabited) divided among three island groups: the Gilbert Islands, the Phoenix Islands, and the Line Islands. The first European to visit the islands, in 1606, was the Spanish explorer Pedro Fernandez de Quiros. The predominantly Micronesian-peopled Gilbert Islands (named after the British sea captain Thomas Gilbert, who arrived there in 1788) and the Melanesian-peopled Ellice Islands became a British protectorate in 1892, and the Gilbert and Ellice Island Colony in 1916. In 1975 the Ellice Islands became the autonomous Tuvalu, the Gilbert Islands attaining self-government in 1977 before becoming independent in 1979 and adopting the name Kiribati (pronounced "Kirribarce," with the emphasis on the first syllable, Kiribati is the "translation" of the English name "Gilbert" into the local Austronesian language).

The flag of Kiribati is based on the arms of the former colony, which, in the colonial flag, appeared on the fly half of the British Blue Ensign. The blue-and-white, wavy lines represent the Pacific Ocean, above which a sun rises against a red sky. The frigate bird, a local bird noted for its power and endurance in flight, soars above the sun.

KUWAIT

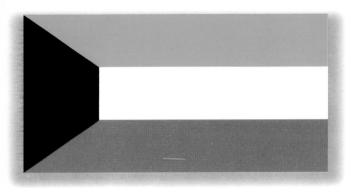

Formal name:
Dawlat al Kuwayt
(State of Kuwait)

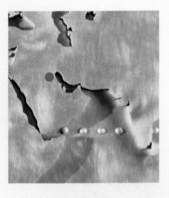

One of the world's smallest countries, Kuwait was part of the Turkish Ottoman Empire from the 16th century, in 1756 the ruling Sabah family founding the sheikhdom of Kuwait that continues to this day. Before oil was discovered during the 1930s, Kuwait's economy was based on pearl-fishing and long-distance trade. A treaty between Sheikh Mubarak al-Sabah and Britain in 1889 made Kuwait a British protectorate until it achieved independence in 1961.

Until independence, the flag of Kuwait, like most of those of the Persian Gulf states, was red and white (Britain requested this so that friendly nations and their ships could be distinguished from those of the many pirates who operated in the Persian Gulf). A strong supporter of the Arab cause in general, in 1961 Kuwait adopted the current flag of green, white, and red horizontal stripes, with a black trapezoid in the hoist. Although the colors are Pan-Arab, they were also inspired by a poem written by Safie Al-Deen Al-Hili and represent the sands whirled up by Kuwaiti horsemen during the battles for freedom (black), Kuwait's meadows (green), the blood of Kuwait's enemies (red), and the pure deeds of the Kuwaiti people (white).

Capital city:
Al Kuwayt (Kuwait City)

Location:
Southwest Asia

Currency:
1 Kuwaiti dinar = 1000 fils

Languages:
Arabic, English

Religions:
Sunni Muslim, Shi'ite Muslim

Flag adopted:
September 7, 1961

Flag ratio:
1:2

Formal name:
Kyrgyz Respublikasy
(Kyrgyz Republic)

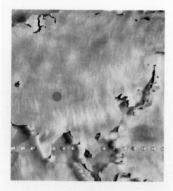

Capital city:
Bishkek

Location:
Central Asia

Currency:
1 rouble = 100 kopecks

Languages:
Kyrghzy, Russian

Religion:
Muslim

Flag adopted:
March 3, 1992

Flag ratio:
3:5

The Kirghiz (a Turkic people) are said to be the descendants of the Mongol invaders who swept across central Asia from the 13th century. Although they were nominally subject to the Uzbek khans (rulers), the horse-breeding, mountain-dwelling, nomadic Kirghiz people retained their independence until 1864, when Russia annexed the area that is today known as Kyrgyzstan. Increasing opposition to Russian rule culminated in a major revolt in 1916, guerrilla activity continuing until after the Bolshevik Revolution of 1917, when Kirghizia became part of an independent Turkestan republic. In 1924, it became the Kara-Kirghiz Autonomous Republic ("Kara," which means "black," was dropped from the name in 1925) and then a Soviet republic from 1936.

Although the present name of Kyrgyzstan was adopted in 1990, some ten months before the U.S.S.R. was dissolved in 1991, the new, post-communist flag was not adopted until 1992. The red of the field is said to have been the color of the banner of the national hero, Manas, who united 40 tribes to form the Kyrgyz nation. In the center of the flag is a circular, stylized representation of the roof of a *yurt* (tent), the traditional home of the nomadic people. This is surrounded by 40 golden sunrays, one for each tribe.

LAOS

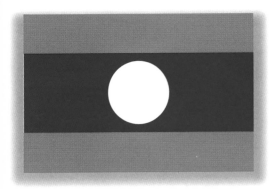

Formal name:
*Sathalanalat Paxathipatai
Paxaxon Loa*
(Loa People's Democratic
Republic)

Part of the Khmer Empire during the 11th century, during the 12th century the area that we today know as Laos was invaded by Buddhist Lao people from Thailand, who established small, independent kingdoms. These were consolidated into an independent kingdom during the 14th century, which was first visited by Europeans during the 17th century. Having become part of French Indochina in 1893, in 1950 the country became semiautonomous under the rulership of the king of Louangprabang, gaining full independence in 1953. Civil war followed until 1975, however, when the communist *Pathet Lao* ("Patriotic Front," subsequently renamed the Lao People's Front) seized power and declared a people's democratic republic.

The royal government's flag that was used from 1952 until 1975 featured a triple-headed elephant on a pedestal, symbolizing the ancient name of the country, the "Land of a Million Elephants." The new national flag of Laos that was introduced in 1975 was that of the *Pathet Lao*, and one of the few not to use the five-pointed socialist star as an emblem. A white, centrally placed disk instead represents the full moon over the Mekong River, symbolizing the unification of the country. The red horizontal stripes signify the blood shed in the fight for freedom, while the central blue stripe denotes the prosperity of the country.

Capital city:
Vientiane

Location:
Southeast Asia

Currency:
1 kip = 100 at

Language:
Lao

Religion:
Buddhist

Flag adopted:
December 2, 1975

Flag ratio:
2:3

LATVIA

Formal name:
Latvijas Republika
(Republic of Latvia)

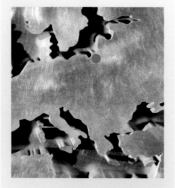

Capital city:
Riga

Location:
Northern Europe

Currency:
1 lats = 100 santimu

Languages:
Latvian, Russian, Lithuanian,
Polish

Religions:
Lutheran, Roman Catholic,
Eastern Orthodox, Jewish

Flag adopted:
February 27, 1990

Flag ratio:
1:2

The area now known as Latvia has, in its past, been ruled by Vikings, Russians, German Teutonic knights, Poland, Lithuania, and Sweden before coming under the control of czarist Russia during the 19th century. The anti-Russian independence movement that had emerged during the late 19th century having grown increasingly strong, Latvia proclaimed itself an independent republic in 1918. In February 1919, however, the Red Army invaded Latvia and began to establish a Soviet-sponsored regime. In 1940, during World War II, Latvia was annexed and became a republic of the U.S.S.R. Latvia again declared its independence in 1990, which was accepted by the U.S.S.R. shortly before its breakup in 1991.

The flag that the newly independent country adopted was the red-and-white-striped flag that was traditionally associated with Latvia. According to legend, this flag had been used in a battle against Estonian troops in 1280; another legend tells of a wounded Latvian fighter who had been wrapped in a white sheet: where he was lying remained white, but the two edges that had been folded over him were stained with his blood. The red of the flag therefore symbolizes Latvian blood shed in the cause of freedom. Although the flag was officially adopted in 1918, its use was suppressed during the period of Soviet rulership. Having reemerged as a result of the revival of Latvian nationalism in the 1980s, it eventually replaced the Soviet Latvian flag in 1990.

LEBANON

Formal name:
A *Jumhuriyah al-Lubnaniyah*
(Lebanese Republic)

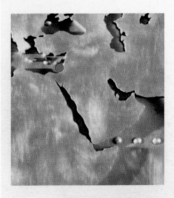

Lebanon was once the home of the ancient Phoenicians, a nation of great seafarers who colonized much of the Mediterranean and developed the first alphabet. It subsequently came under Egyptian, Assyrian, Persian, Roman, and Byzantine rule until 1516, when the Ottoman Empire began to rule it as part of Syria. After World War I, France governed Lebanon under a League of Nations' mandate until the country became an independent republic in 1943.

During the period of French rule, the Lebanese flag was a French *Tricolore* with the emblem of a tree positioned in the central, white stripe. In an effort to create a flag that was neutral, as well as neither Christian or Muslim, the blue of the French flag was subsequently removed, the remaining red and white bands then being turned to the horizontal and the red band being split in two. On the central white band was placed the green Cedar of Lebanon, the country's symbol for 2,000 years and also an emblem used by the Lebanese Maronite Christians during the 18th century. The official symbolism of the flag is, however, that the red signifies the blood shed in the cause of freedom, the white symbolizes peace, while the green denotes immortality.

Capital city:
Bayrut (Beirut)

Location:
Southwest Asia

Currency:
1 Lebanese pound
= 100 piastres

Languages:
Arabic, French, English

Religions:
Muslim, Christian

Flag adopted:
December 7, 1943

Flag ratio:
2:3

Formal name:
'Muso oa Lesotho
(Kingdom of Lesotho)

Capital city:
Maseru

Location:
Southern Africa

Currency:
1 loti = 100 lisente

Languages:
Sesotho (a Bantu language),
English

Religions:
Roman Catholic, Protestant

Flag adopted:
January 20, 1987

Flag ratio:
2:3

Lesotho is one of only two nations in the world to be completely encircled by another country (the other is San Marino). The nation was founded as Basutoland by the Sotho leader, Moshoeshoe I (c.1790–1870), in 1827. Having escaped being incorporated into South Africa (which surrounds it, and on which it depends economically) by becoming a British protectorate in 1868, it achieved internal self-government in 1965 as the kingdom of Lesotho (with Moshoeshoe II as its king) and was granted full independence in 1966.

The first flag to be adopted by the newly independent Lesotho was based on the colors of the Basotho National Party (which led the country to independence) and featured a Basotho straw hat. Following a military coup (1986), a new flag was adopted in 1987 that made no reference to any political party at all, instead using colors that are symbolic of the national motto: *Khotos-Pula-Nala,* which means "Peace (white), Rain (blue), and Plenty (green)." In the canton is the silhouette of the national coat of arms – a crossed *assegai* (barbed spear), knobkerrie (club), and a traditional Basotho shield (which in reality has a plumed spine) – symbols of the people's willingness to defend their independence.

LIBERIA

The area in West Africa known as Liberia was bought in 1821 by the American Colonization Society, a philanthropic group whose aim was to establish a new homeland for liberated black slaves from the southern United States. The first settlers arrived in 1822, and Liberia was declared an independent republic in 1847.

Liberia's colonial flag was based on the U.S.'s "Stars and Stripes," but with a "Christian" cross in the canton, its 11 stripes representing the 11 signatories of Liberia's declaration of independence and constitution. The new flag of the republic, sewn by a special committee headed by Susanna Waring-Lewis, was unfurled in 1847. Although similar to the colonial flag in that it had 11 red and white stripes, in place of the cross in the canton there was now a star. The canton itself is now said to symbolize the continent of Africa, the five-pointed star, which recalls the fact that Liberia was the first independent African republic, giving the flag its official name: "The Lone Star." The flag's colors represent valor (red), purity (white), and fidelity (blue).

Formal name:
Republic of Liberia

Capital city:
Monrovia

Location:
West Africa

Currency:
1 Liberian dollar = 100 cents

Language:
English

Religions:
Muslim, Christian, diverse traditional beliefs

Flag adopted:
July 24, 1847

Flag ratio:
10:19

Formal name:
Al Jamahiriyal al-Arabiyah al-Libiyah ash Shabiyah Ishtirakiya
(Socialist People's Libyan Arab Jamahiriya)

Capital city:
Tarabulus (Tripoli)

Location:
North Africa

Currency:
1 Libyan dinar = 1000 dirhams

Language:
Arabic

Religion:
Muslim

Flag adopted:
November 19, 1977

Flag ratio:
1:2

Inhabited by North-African nomads, and ruled successively by the Phoenicians, Greeks, Romans, and Byzantines, the area now known as Libya became part of the Ottoman Empire during the 16th century. Having been conquered by Italy in 1911, at the end of World War II it was divided into three provinces: Tripolitania, Cyrenaica (both under British control), and Fezzan (administered by the French). The country became independent as the United Kingdom of Libya, ruled by King Idris, in 1951. Following a bloodless coup in 1969, however, nationalist army officers led by Colonel Moamer al-Khaddhafi, proclaimed a Libyan-Arab republic.

The flag used by Libya between 1951 and 1969 was a horizontal tricolor of black, red, and green, charged with a white crescent and star, all colors that had been flown on the Arab Revolt flag of 1917, the black, red, and green also respectively representing the provinces of Cyrenaica (black), Fezzan (red), and Tripolitania (green). The emblems were dropped from the flag in 1969 and, from 1971 to 1977, when Libya joined with Syria and Egypt to form the Federation of Arab Republics, Libya flew the federation's tricolor flag, which bore a hawk emblem in the center and the country's name beneath it. When Libya quit the federation in 1977, however, it adopted the current plain green flag, symbolizing both Islam and Libya's aim of achieving agricultural self-sufficiency.

LIECHTENSTEIN

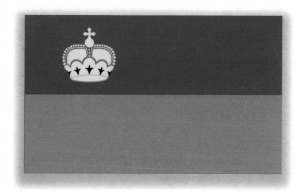

Formal name:
Fürstentum Liechtenstein
(Principality of Liechtenstein)

One of the smallest of the world's independent states, with a total area of just 62 square miles (169 square kilometers), Liechtenstein's boundaries have remained unchanged since 1434. It has been a sovereign state since 1342, although its history as a modern nation dates from 1719, when it acquired its present name and ruling family following the union of the counties of Vaduz and Schellenberg to form the principality of Liechtenstein. Separated from Germany by Austria, Liechtenstein was unique among ethnic German principalities in that it did not become part of the German Empire in 1871. Because of its diminutive size, however, in international matters Liechtenstein has found it useful to associate itself with larger nations: until 1990, when Liechtenstein was admitted to the United Nations, it was represented abroad firstly by Austria (until 1919), and then by Switzerland, with whom it continues to maintain a customs union.

The red and blue colors of the national flag have been in use since the early 19th century, often in a vertical arrangement. Although the stripes were altered to form a horizontal pattern in 1921, the flag so resembled that of Haiti when both were flown at the 1936 Olympic Games in Berlin, Germany, that a crown, signifying Liechtenstein's status as a principality, was added to the canton in the following year.

Capital city:
Vaduz

Location:
Western Europe

Currency:
1 Swiss franc = 100 centimes

Languages:
German (official language),
Alemannish (Swiss-German)

Religion:
Roman Catholic

Flag adopted:
June 24, 1937

Flag ratio:
3:5

LITHUANIA

Formal name:
Lietuvos Respublika
(Republic of Lithuania)

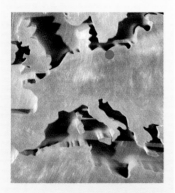

Capital city:
Vilnius

Location:
Northern Europe

Currency:
I litas = 100 centai

Languages:
Lithuanian, Russian, Polish

Religions:
Roman Catholic, Russian
Orthodox, Lutheran

Flag adopted:
March 20, 1989

Flag ratio:
1:2

Lithuania became a unified nation at the end of the 12th century and was subsequently greatly enlarged by the "grand princes" who annexed Byelorussia (Belarus) and the Ukraine. When Grand Prince Jagiello married Queen Jadwiga of Poland in 1386, the two crowns were united, although Lithuania maintained its autonomy until czarist Russia gained control of the region in 1795. Revolts in 1832 and 1863 failed to win independence, and it was only in 1918, following the Russian Revolution, that Lithuania became an autonomous state. Occupied by the Soviet Union in 1940 Lithuania remained under Soviet control until 1991, when it became the first Soviet republic to break with Moscow and declare its independence.

On attaining independence in 1991, Lithuania readopted the tricolor of yellow, green, and red that it had flown between 1918 and 1940, but which had been suppressed following its annexation and occupation by the Soviet Union. The tricolor reappeared in independence rallies in 1988, and in 1989 its use as the national flag was legalized. In 1918, a special commission comprising Jonas Basanavicius, Tadas Daugirdas, and Antanas Zmuidzinavicius had selected these colors. The flags of the ancient Lithuanian grand duchy had been red, and the color was also said to symbolize the blood that had been shed in defense of Lithuania's freedom, while the yellow signified the country's fields of grain, and the green the great forests of the Baltic region.

LUXEMBOURG

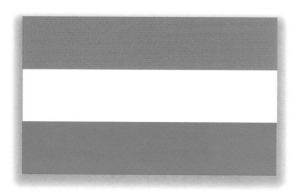

Formal name:
Grand-Duché de Luxembourg
(Grand Duchy of Luxembourg)

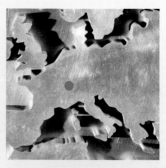

Capital city:
Luxembourg-Ville (Luxembourg
City)

Location:
Western Europe

Currency:
euro, I Luxembourg franc =
100 centimes

Languages:
Letzeburgish (Luxemburgish),
French, German

Religion:
Roman Catholic

Flag adopted:
officially adopted June 23, 1972,
though first hoisted 1845-48

Flag ratio:
3:5

Luxembourg's central location at the "crossroads of Europe" has resulted in it being ruled by many other nations prior to its gaining of full independence in 1848. The House of Luxembourg, which was founded in 1060 by Count Conrad, became a duchy in 1354. Passing to the dukes of Burgundy in 1443, it was inherited by the Spanish Hapsburgs in 1555, being ruled by Austria from 1715 until it was ceded (with Belgium) to France during the Napoleonic Wars. Made a grand duchy in 1815, with the Dutch king, William I, as its sovereign, in 1830, the Belgian provinces of the Netherlands and Luxembourg joined in revolt. Although Belgium became an autonomous kingdom as a result, Luxembourg remained part of it until 1839, when the western part was ceded to Belgium, the remaining portion being reorganized as a sovereign and independent state in 1848.

Luxembourg did not have a flag until 1830, when patriots flew the national colors of red, white, and blue that were derived from the 13th-century arms of the grand duke of Luxembourg. Even though Luxembourg revolted against Dutch rule, the current flags of both nations are similar, although the Luxembourgeois flag is longer than the flag of the Netherlands, and the blue is of a lighter shade.

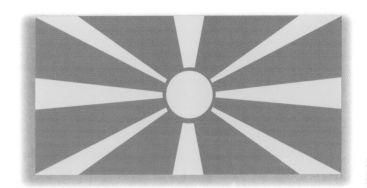

Formal name:
Republika Makedonija
(Republic of Macedonia) [Note:
The designation of the United
Nations is "Former Yugoslav
Republic of Macedonia," a
compromise, as Greece also
has a territory also called
Macedonia.]

Capital city:
Skopje

Location:
Southeastern Europe

Currency:
1 Macedonian dinar
= 100 paras

Languages:
Macedonian, Albanian

Religions:
Macedonian Orthodox, Muslim

Flag adopted:
October 5, 1995

Flag ratio:
1:2

The ancient region of Macedonia – of which the present-day republic comprises only a part – was settled by the Slavs during the 6th century. It was subsequently conquered by the Bulgars, Byzantium, Serbia, and the Ottoman Empire before being divided up between Greece, Bulgaria, and Serbia in 1913. After World War I, Serbian Macedonia – which constitutes today's present state – became part of the federal state of Yugoslavia.

As part of Yugoslavia, Macedonia's flag was red, with a gold-fimbriated, red star in the canton. The first flag to be adopted by Macedonia on its declaration of independence in 1991 was a red flag charged with the "Star of Virjina," which was based on a symbol found in the tomb of Philip of Macedonia (the father of Alexander the Great) at Virjina. Following objections from Greece (which claimed that it was a wholly Greek symbol), in 1995 Macedonia adopted its current flag, which consists of a red field bearing a golden-yellow sun from which emanate eight rays that thicken toward the ends.

MADAGASCAR

Formal name:
*Repoblika Demokratika n'i
Madagaskar*
(Democratic Republic of
Madagascar)

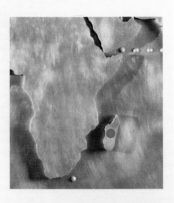

Madagascar is made up of Madagascar Island – the fourth-largest island in the world – as well as a number of smaller islands that lie in the Indian Ocean, off the southeastern coast of Africa. Madagascar's first inhabitants are thought to have been Southeast Asians from Indonesia, who arrived during the early centuries A.D., soon being followed by mainland Africans and subsequently Arabs. Attracted by its valuable, hardwood forests, Europeans began visiting the islands during the 1500s, although attempts by the Portuguese, Dutch, and English to colonize them were constantly thwarted by the islanders' fierce resistance. Madagascar was divided into small kingdoms until the 19th century, when, assisted by foreign traders and missionaries, the islands were united within the kingdom of the highland Merina people. Having been annexed by France in 1896, Madagascar's strong resistance to its colonial ruler throughout the 20th century resulted in its full independence in 1960.

The flag of Madagascar was introduced in 1958, when the country achieved self-rule, and consists of a vertical, white band in the hoist, adjacent to which are horizontal bands of red and green. While red and white were the traditional colors of the Merina, green is said to represent the island's other ethnic group, the *cotiers* ("coastal people"), the former peasant class.

Capital city:
Antananarivo

Location:
Indian Ocean/Southeastern
coast of Africa

Currency:
1 Malagasy franc
= 100 centimes

Languages:
Malagasy, French

Religions:
Animist, Christian, Muslim

Flag adopted:
October 14, 1958

Flag ratio:
2:3

MALAWI

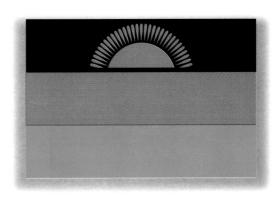

Formal name:
Mfuko la Malawi
(Republic of Malawi)

Capital city:
Lilongwe

Location:
Southeast Africa

Currency:
1 Malawi kwacha
= 100 tambala

Languages:
English (official language),
Chichewa (national language),
diverse Bantu languages

Religions:
Christian, Muslim, Animist

Flag adopted:
July 6, 1964

Flag ratio:
2:3

From the 15th to 19th centuries, warfare between the rival Yao and Ngoni peoples, coupled with the difficult terrain of the county, prevented Malawi from being infiltrated by foreigners. The explorer Dr. David Livingstone reached Lake Nyasa ("Nyasa" means "lake" in Chichewa, so it was really called "Lake Lake" until being renamed Lake Malawi) in 1859. Britain annexed the region in 1891, in 1907 designating it the Protectorate of Nyasaland. Malawi was part of the Federation of Rhodesia and Nyasaland (now modern-day Zimbabwe, Zambia, and Malawi) from 1953 until 1963, when, partly as a result of a campaign for independence led by the Malawi Congress Party (M.C.P.), the federation was dissolved. Having proclaimed its independence in 1964, in 1966 Malawi became a republic.

The colors of the Malawi flag are the same as those of the M.C.P., whose flag was derived from the red, black, and green tricolor of the "Back-to-Africa" activist Marcus Garvey. The colors symbolize the African people (black), the blood of the freedom-fighters (red), and the fertility of the land (green). "Malawi" means "Flaming Waters," a name that alludes to the reflection of the sun on Lake Malawi, a symbolism that is reflected in the appearance on the national flag of a *kwacha* (rising sun).

MALAYSIA

Formal name:
Persekutuan Malaysia
(Federation of Malaysia)

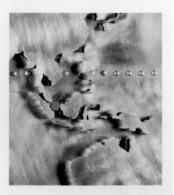

Malaysia's ethnic diversity reflects its complex history, its wealth and strategic position having attracted numerous peoples to its shores. From the 9th to the 14th centuries, it was part of the Buddhist kingdom of Srivijaya before falling to the Hindu Javanese. Islam reached the region during the 15th century, while the spice trade attracted Dutch, Portuguese, and British interests. British rule was progressively established during the 19th and 20th centuries, that is, until 1957, when Malaya (as it was then called) became independent, the Federation of Malaysia being formed in 1963.

Independent Malaysia's first flag was based on the "Stars and Stripes." Called *Jular Gemilang* ("Glorious Stripes"), it consisted of 11 red and white stripes and a blue canton charged with a golden Islamic crescent and 11-pointed star (the number of stripes and points denoting the equal status of the 11 states of the federation). In 1963, three new states – Sabah, Sarawak, and Singapore – joined the federation, causing the flag's stripes and star-points to be increased to 14. Although Singapore left the federation in 1965, this flag was retained, the fourteenth stripe now being said to symbolize the federated district of Kuala Lumpur, while the 14 star-points denote the unity of the states and the federal government.

Capital city:
Kuala Lumpur

Location:
Southeast Asia

Currency:
1 ringgit = 100 cents

Languages:
Bahasa Malay, Chinese, Tamil,
English

Religions:
Muslim, Buddhist, Hindu

Flag adopted:
September 16, 1963

Flag ratio:
1:2

Formal name:
Dehevi Jumhuriyya
(Republic of the Maldives)

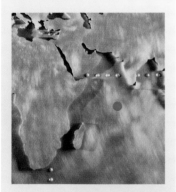

Capital city:
Malé

Location:
Indian Ocean

Currency:
1 Maldivian rufiyaa = 100 laari

Language:
Dihevi

Religion:
Muslim

Flag adopted:
July 26, 1965

Flag ratio:
2:3

The Maldives is a group of 1,196 islands in the Indian Ocean, about 400 miles (640 kilometers) southwest of Sri Lanka. Known locally as "The Thousand Islands," only 203 of the coral islands are inhabited. Originally settled by Buddhist peoples from Asia, the islands came under Muslim control during the 12th century before the onset of Portuguese rule in 1518. A dependency of Ceylon (now Sri Lanka) from 1645 to 1948, the Maldive Islands, as they were then known, were a British protectorate from 1887 to 1965. Following the proclamation of a republic in 1953, the sultan was restored in 1954, but in 1968, three years after the country had gained its independence as the Maldives, the islands reverted to their republican status.

During the early 20th century, the flag of the Maldives was red, with a white crescent facing the hoist in reflection of the region's Islamic culture. When the Maldives became independent of Ceylon in 1948, the crescent was turned to face the opposite direction and was set within a green panel (green is the traditional color of the Prophet Muhammad, as well as signifying peace and prosperity). Although a pattern of black and white diagonals was also added to the hoist, this was removed when independence was achieved in 1965.

MALI

Formal name:
République de Mali
(Republic of Mali)

From the 4th to the 11th centuries, Mali was part of the ancient kingdom of Ghana and subsequently of the Muslim Mali Empire, which occupied much of Northwest Africa between the 7th and 15th centuries. Although the powerful Muslim Songhai Empire ruled the region during the 16th century, in 1591 forces from Morocco, who were seeking control of the Sudanese gold trade, invaded, leaving the area divided into small kingdoms. Mali's inland location meant that it did not become the subject of European interest – which was largely confined to coastal trading centers – until the 19th century, when treaties made between local rulers and the French led to Mali becoming part of the colony of French Sudan in 1895. In 1959, it formed the Federation of Mali with Senegal, and when Senegal left the federation in 1960, Mali became a fully independent republic.

The colors of the federation's flag, which Mali continued to use until 1961, were those that had first been adopted by Ghana (the Pan-African colors of green, yellow, and red), although they were arranged vertically in Mali's flag, in the manner of the French *Tricolore*. Within the central yellow stripe was a *kanaga*, a stylized human figure. In March 1961, following pressure from Muslims, who objected to representational images of the human shape, the black *kanaga* symbol was dropped.

Capital city:
Bamako

Location:
West Africa

Currency:
1 C.F.A. franc = 100 centimes

Languages:
French, Bambara, Songhai

Religion:
Muslim, Animist

Flag adopted:
March 1, 1961

Flag ratio:
2:3

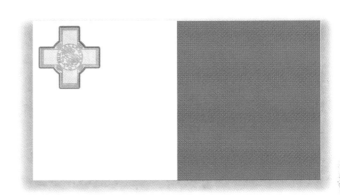

Formal name:
Repubblika ta'Malta
(Republic of Malta)

Capital city:
Valletta

Location:
Southern Europe

Currency:
1 Maltese lira = 100 cents =
1000 mils

Languages:
Maltese, English, Italian

Religion:
Roman Catholic

Flag adopted:
September 21, 1964

Flag ratio:
2:3

Malta's strategic location in the Mediterranean Sea caused it to be occupied by Phoenicians, Greeks, Carthaginians, Romans, and Arabs before Roger of Sicily conquered the islands in 1090, after which they remained under Sicilian rule for some centuries. A key stronghold during the Crusades, in 1530 the Holy Roman Emperor Charles V gave the islands to the knights of St. John of Jerusalem. Napoleon having ended the knights' rule in 1798, the islands were annexed by the British in 1814, subsequently becoming an important base for the Royal Navy. Having endured heavy bombing raids by the Axis forces during World War II, Malta's valor was rewarded with the George Cross, a British bravery award. Malta became independent in 1964.

According to myth, the red and white, horizontal bands of the Maltese flag were originally squares that Roger of Sicily cut from his own checkered flag. It is more likely, however, that the colors were derived from the arms of the knights of Malta, a white Maltese cross on a red shield. During British colonial rule, Malta's flag bore a red-and-white shield device, to which a blue canton containing the George Cross medal was added in 1943. The blue canton was removed on Malta's independence, a narrow, red fimbriation being added to the George Cross.

MARSHALL ISLANDS

Formal name:
Republic of the Marshall Islands

The Marshall Islands are made up of two groups of coral islands and atolls: the northern, Ralik chain (11 islands) and the southern, Rattak chain (13 islands). Although first sighted by Europeans during the 16th century, it was only in 1906 that the islands were colonized, by Germany. From 1919 to 1946 they were administered by Japan, passing to the United States in 1946 as part of the Pacific Trust Territory. The islands of Bikini and Eniwetok subsequently made the Marshall Islands internationally famous because it was here that the U.S. tested atomic and hydrogen bombs between 1946 and 1963. Having become a self-governing territory in 1979, in 1991 the Marshall Islands gained full independence.

The national flag, which was first adopted in 1979, was designed by Emlain Kabua, the president's wife. The blue field represents the Pacific Ocean, while the white and orange bands represent the Rattak (sunrise) and Ralik (sunset) chains respectively. The colors are also traditional, symbolizing bravery (orange) and peace (white). The star signifies the Christian faith, its 24 points representing both the islands' geographical location just above the equator and their 24 municipal districts. The four main points represent the major centers of Majuro, Ebeye, Jaluit, and Wotje.

Capital city:
Dalap-Uliga-Darrit (Majuro)

Location:
Pacific Ocean

Currency:
1 U.S. dollar = 100 cents

Languages:
Marshallese, English

Religions:
Protestant, Roman Catholic

Flag adopted:
May 1, 1979

Flag ratio:
10:19

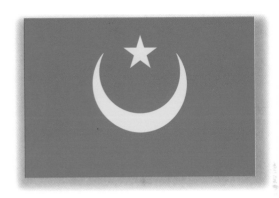

Formal name:
Al Jumhuriyah al Islamiyah al Muritaniyah
(Islamic Republic of Mauritania)

Capital city:
Nouakchott

Location:
Northwest Africa

Currency:
1 Mauritanian ouguiya = 5 khoums

Languages:
Arabic (official language), Poular, Wolof, Soninke (national languages)

Religion:
Muslim

Flag adopted:
April 1, 1959

Flag ratio:
2:3

Mauritania was the name first given to the Roman province (most of which lies in the Sahara Desert) in Northwest Africa inhabited by the Mauri, a Berber people. Having come under the rule of Ghana during the 7th century, the Berbers were converted to Islam during the 8th century. The Arab influence continued to dominate the region, even after the French arrived to trade in gum arabic. Part of the colony of French West Africa from 1920, Mauritania achieved self-government in 1958 and full independence in 1960.

The national flag was adopted after Mauritania became autonomous, some commentators asserting that the design was selected by Mouktar Ould Daddah, the leader of the Mauritanian People's Party (P.P.M.) and the first president of the independent Mauritania. The flag emphasizes both the country's African location and its official faith, Islam. As well as being Pan-African colors, the green and gold additionally symbolize Mauritania's hopes for a bright future (green) and the sands of the Sahara Desert (gold). The crescent symbol is an Islamic emblem, while green is known as the "color of the Prophet" (Muhammad). All in all, the flag is a symbolic expression of the country's formal name, the Islamic Republic of Mauritania.

135

MAURITIUS

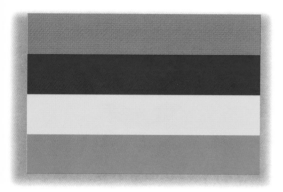

Formal name:
Republik Morisiê
(Republic of Mauritius)

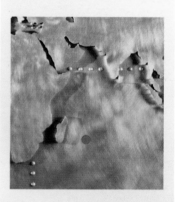

Perhaps surprisingly, although Mauritius was known to Arab and Portuguese seafarers, it, along with its outlying islands of Rodrigues and the Agalega Islands, remained uninhabited until 1598, when the Dutch established a small-scale colony and named the island after the *stadholder* (chief magistrate) of the Netherlands, Prince Maurice of Nassau. The Dutch having abandoned their venture in 1710, the French took possession of Mauritius in 1715, bringing in slaves from Africa to work the sugar plantations, and renaming it the Île de France. Captured by the British in 1810 during the Napoleonic Wars, Mauritius became a British colony in 1814. The abolition of slavery in 1833 brought about the importation of indentured laborers from India, whose descendants now constitute some 70 percent of all Mauritians, the rest of the population being largely Creole (of mixed African and European descent). Mauritius achieved self-government in 1957 and full independence in 1968.

The national flag, which was designed by the British College of Arms prior to independence, uses the colors found on the arms that were granted Mauritius in 1906. The colors are symbolic: the red symbolizes Mauritius's independence, the blue its location in the Indian Ocean, the green its lush vegetation, and the yellow the people's bright hopes for their country's future.

Capital city:
Port Louis

Location:
South Indian Ocean

Currency:
1 Mauritian rupee = 100 cents

Languages:
English (official language),
French, Hindi, Creole, Bjojpuri

Religions:
Hindu, Roman Catholic, Muslim

Flag adopted:
January 9, 1968

Flag ratio:
2:3

Formal name:
Estados Unidos Méxicanos
(United Mexican States)

Capital city:
Mexico City

Location:
North America

Currency:
1 Mexican peso = 100 centavos

Languages:
Spanish, Nahuatl

Religion:
Roman Catholic

Flag adopted:
November 2, 1821

Flag ratio:
4:7

Many civilizations originated in Mexico, including the Olmec, Maya, Toltec, Mixtec, Zapotec, and Aztec, the Aztecs settling on Mexico's high, central plateau. The last Aztec king, Montezuma II, having been killed in 1520, during the Spanish conquest of the region, the Viceroyalty of New Spain was established in 1535. Having found colonial rule increasingly oppressive, the Mexicans began their struggle for independence in 1810, achieving their aim in 1821.

The flag that was used by Mexico's liberation army was inspired by the revolutionary French *Tricolore*, although the colors of its vertical stripes are those of the liberation army, the green symbolizing hope, the white unity, purity, and honesty, and the red the blood of national heroes. The state emblem of Mexico – an eagle and a snake – which dates from independence, was added in 1968 to distinguish the flag from Italy's tricolor. The emblem recalls a legend telling how the god Huitzilopochtli exhorted the Aztecs to seek a place where an eagle had landed on a prickly-pear cactus to eat a snake. After centuries of wandering, the Aztecs found the sign that they had been searching for on a swampy island in Lake Texcoco, building their new home, which they named Tenochtitlán ("Place of the Prickly-Pear Cactus") on the site in A.D. 1325, now occupied by the modern Mexico City, .

MICRONESIA

Formal name:
Federated States of Micronesia

The Pacific Ocean islands are divided into three groups: Polynesia (islands from the Hawaiian Islands south to New Zealand), Melanesia (islands in the South Pacific, northeast of Australia), and Micronesia (islands lying north of the equator and east of the Philippines). Micronesia – whose main island groups are Palau, the Caroline Islands, the Mariana Islands, and the Marshall Islands – was part of the United Nations' Trust Territory of the Pacific Islands that was established in 1945 and administered by the United States.

Although a Micronesian flag, flying the colors of the United Nations, has been in use since 1962, the number of stars has varied. In 1962 there were six stars, representing Palau, the Marshall Islands, the Mariana Islands, Ponape, Truk, and Yap (in the Carolines). In 1976, the Mariana Islands (now the Northern Mariana Islands) left the Micronesian federation after gaining U.S. Overseas' Territory status, the state of Kosaie, formed in 1977, subsequently joining the federation. The Micronesian flag was altered in 1978, when the Marshall Islands and Palau left the federation, the number of stars being reduced to four. Arranged like the points of a compass, they represent the remaining states of Chuuk (Truk), Kosrae (Kusaie), Yap, and Pohnpei (Ponape), which together constitute independent Micronesia.

Capital city:
Palikir

Location:
Pacific Ocean

Currency:
1 U.S. dollar = 100 cents

Language:
English

Religion:
Christian

Flag adopted:
November 30, 1978

Flag ratio:
10:19

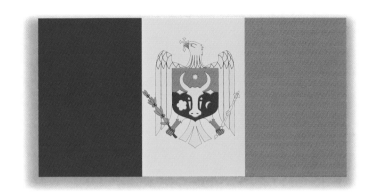

Formal name:
Republica Moldova
(Republic of Moldova)

Capital city:
Kishinev (Chisinau)

Location:
Eastern Europe

Currency:
1 Moldovian leu = 100 bani

Languages:
Romanian, Ukrainian, Russian

Religion:
Eastern (Moldovian) Orthodox

Flag adopted:
May 12, 1990

Flag ratio:
2:3

Moldova has also been known as Bessarabia (from the 10th to the 12th centuries, when the area was ruled by the Kiev Rus) and Moldavia (from the 15th century, when it was a Romanian principality within the Ottoman Empire). In 1812, it was ceded to the Russians, who remained in control until 1917, when a short-lived Bessarabian Republic was created, only to be crushed by a Bolshevik invasion in 1918, after which the region became part of the kingdom of Romania. In 1944, following a Soviet invasion, it became the Moldavian Soviet Republic, becoming the independent Republic of Moldova following the dissolution of the U.S.S.R. in 1991.

Moldova's tricolor (which is almost identical to Romania's flag) was first adopted in 1848, the year in which revolutions raged throughout Europe, when the colors represented the three Ottoman provinces of Moldavia (red), Oltenia (East Wallachia, blue), and Muntenia (West Wallachia, yellow). Today, the colors are said to denote Moldova's past, present, and future. Positioned within the yellow stripe are the Moldovan arms, a golden eagle holding an Orthodox Christian cross in its beak and an olive branch and scepter in its talons. On top of the eagle is a shield divided in half horizontally which features the head of an auroch (a now extinct, European bison), as well as astrological emblems, all of which symbolize Moldova.

MONACO

Formal name:
Principauté de Monaco
(Principality of Monaco)

Bordering the Mediterranean Sea, Monaco is an independent principality that forms an enclave within Southeastern France. Although a mere 0.75 square mile (1.95 square kilometers) in size, Monaco is one of the world's most densely populated states. The principality was established in 1297 by the House of Grimaldi, which continues to rule Monaco to this day. (Legend says that the Grimaldi were able to enter and conquer the fortified city because their soldiers were disguised as monks.) Monaco was annexed by French forces during the French Revolution, the Grimaldi being imprisoned (one was guillotined) before being restored to power in 1814 under the protection of the king of Sardinia. Annexed again by France in 1848, Monaco lost much territory to its neighbor, who considered it part of Italy. Monaco's relations with both France and Italy have nevertheless always been close: since 1861, Monaco has enjoyed French protection, while the Grimaldi family came originally from Genoa, Italy, and the language of the Monégasques (as the citizens of Monaco are known) is a mixture of French and Italian.

The simple, red-over-white bicolor of Monaco was adopted in 1881. Derived from the Grimaldi family's arms, which feature a red-and-white-checkered shield, the bicolor replaced the previous flag, which had been a white field charged with the same shield, as well as a crown.

Capital city:
Monaco-Ville

Location:
Southwestern Europe

Currency:
1 French franc = 100 centimes

Languages:
French, Monégasque

Religion:
Roman Catholic

Flag adopted:
April 4, 1881

Flag ratio:
4:5

Formal name:
Mogol Uls
(Republic of Mongolia)

Capital city:
Ulaanbaatar (Ulan Bator)

Location:
East Asia

Currency:
1 tugrik = 100 möngö

Languages:
Khalkha Mongolian, Kazkh,
Russian

Religions:
Buddhist, Muslim, Shamanist,
Russian Orthodox

Flag adopted:
February 12, 1912

Flag ratio:
1:2

Originally inhabited by nomads from Northern Asia, in 1206 Mongolia was united under Genghis Khan, forming part of the Mongol Empire by the end of the 13th century. Although "Outer" Mongolia, in the north, retained its autonomy as a Buddhist monarchy, from 1689 "Inner Mongolia" was controlled by China. Mongolia became autonomous in 1911, nationalists forming the Mongolian People's Republic in 1924.

Mongolia's flag features the republic's national emblem, the *soyombo*, which is based on ancient Mongolian and Buddhist symbols. At the top is a fire symbol, representing the family hearth and the Mongolian people, its three flames signifying the past, present, and future. Below this are symbols of the sun and moon, referring to Mongolia's Shamanistic traditions. Two triangles represent arrows or spears pointing to the ground, denoting "death to the enemies," while two rectangles represent a fortress and symbolize Mongolia's strength as a nation. In Mongolian symbolism, the yin-yang circle that appears within the emblem represents a fish, signifying reason and wisdom (because fish never close their eyes). This emblem was placed centrally on the flag between 1924 and 1940, being moved to the hoist during the period of communist rule, when a socialist star, along with a central blue stripe, was added. The star was removed in 1992.

MOROCCO

Formal name:
Al Mamlakah al Maghribiyah
(Kingdom of Morocco)

Originally inhabited by Berbers, Morocco was conquered by Arabs during the 7th century. United from the 11th century under the Almoravids, who ruled a Muslim empire that included Morocco, Algeria, and Spain, the Almoravids were followed by the Almohads, whose empire extended to Libya and Tunisia. During the 16th and 17th centuries the Sharifian Dynasty, which claims decent from the Prophet Muhammad, rose to power, and continues to occupy the Moroccan throne today. Divided into French and Spanish protectorates in 1912, Morocco became fully independent as the Sultanate of Morocco in 1956, the former Spanish protectorate, along with Tangier (previously an international zone), joining the former French protectorate to form the new state. The sultan was restyled "king" in 1957.

During the 16th century Moroccan flags were plain red, denoting the blood ties between the sultans and the Prophet Muhammad. In 1915, during the reign of Mulay Yussuf, the green-outlined, five-pointed star known as the "Seal of Solomon" was added to the red field. This flag was retained during the period of French and Spanish administration (although it was restricted to use on land) and was reconfirmed when Morocco achieved its own independence.

Capital city:
Rabat

Location:
Northwest Africa

Currency:
1 dirham = 100 centimes

Languages:
Arabic, Berber, French

Religion:
Muslim

Flag adopted:
November 17, 1915

Flag ratio:
2:3

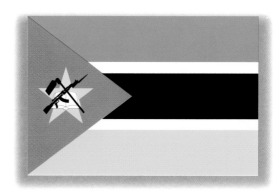

Formal name:
República de Moçambique
(Republic of Mozambique)

Capital city:
Maputo

Location:
Southeast Africa

Currency:
1 metical = 100 centavos

Languages:
Portuguese, Bantu

Religions:
Roman Catholic, Muslim,
Animist

Flag adopted:
May 1, 1983

Flag ratio:
2:3

Mozambique's coast first attracted foreign settlers during the 9th century, when Arab traders arrived in the Bantu people's land. The Portuguese colonized Mozambique in 1505, exploiting its resources of gold and ivory and enslaving its people, whom they transported to sugar plantations in Cuba and Brazil.

Groups opposed to Portuguese rule united during the 1960s to form the Front for the Liberation of Mozambique (*Frente de Liberação do Moçambique*, or F.R.E.L.I.M.O.), whose flag flew the Pan-African colors arranged as green, red, and black horizontal stripes, with white fimbriations and a red triangle in the hoist. This was the flag that was temporarily adopted when Mozambique attained its independence in 1974. (During its colonial period, Mozambique did not fly a flag, Portugal considering its colonies to be an integral part of it.) On the first official flag of Mozambique, the stripes formed four irregular triangles radiating from the upper hoist, which contained a white cogwheel (for industry), a crossed hoe (denoting agriculture), and a Kalashnikov rifle (signifying defense) positioned over an open book (symbolizing education), as well as a small, red star (representing socialism). During the early 1980s, the horizontally striped format was reintroduced and the country's arms were placed on a yellow star within the red triangle, the cogwheel device being dropped, and the yellow star of Marxism being enlarged, in 1983.

MYANMAR

Until 1989, Myanmar was known as Burma. The Burmese arrived from the region where China and Tibet meet in A.D. 638 and, by 850, the Burmese had organized a great Burmese state within the Irawaddy Valley. Following a series of wars with Britain, Burma became a province of India from 1886 to 1937, and a British crown colony until 1948, when it gained full independence.

The Myanmar flag has its origins in the banner of the resistance movement, a red flag charged with a white star, that fought against occupying Japanese forces during World War II. At independence, the flag was altered to a red field with a blue canton, with five small stars (representing the ethnic diversity of the country) surrounding a large star (symbolizing national unity). In 1974, when Burma became the Socialist Republic of the Burmese Federation, the emblem was altered to 14 stars (one for each of the federated states) surrounding a cogwheel and ears of rice (representing the union of industry and agriculture). The flag's colors symbolize the people's courage (red), peace (blue), and virtue (white). Although Burma changed its name to the Union of Myanmar in 1989, it did not change its flag.

Formal name:
*Pyiduangsu Myanma
Naingngandaw*
(Union of Myanmar)

Capital city:
Yangon (Rangoon)

Location:
South Asia

Currency:
1 Myanmar kyat = 100 pyas

Language:
Burmese

Religion:
Buddhist

Flag adopted:
January 3, 1974

Flag ratio:
5:9

Formal name:
Republic of Namibia

Capital city:
Windhock

Location:
Southwest Africa

Currency:
1 Namibian dollar = 100 cents

Languages:
English, Afrikaans, German

Religion:
Protestant

Flag adopted:
March 21, 1990

Flag ratio:
2:3

Originally inhabited first by the Damara people and subsequently by the Khoikoi, Ovambo, and Herero, Bartolomeu Diaz was the first European to visit Namibia in 1448. The region was established as *Deutsch Südwestafrika* (German Southwest Africa) in 1884, despite strong resistance (an unsuccessful revolt from 1904 to 1908 leading to some 50,000 Herero deaths). South Africa conquered the territory in 1915 and was granted a League of Nations' mandate to govern it in 1920. Although the United Nations canceled the mandate in 1966, South Africa ignored the ruling, Namibia eventually being liberated in 1990, following a campaign of guerrilla warfare led by the nationalist South West African People's Organization (S.W.A.P.O.).

The flag adopted by Namibia at independence, which was derived from 835 designs submitted by the public to the National Symbols Committee, used the colors of both S.W.A.P.O. (blue, red, and green) and the second major political party, the Democratic Turnhalle Alliance (red, white, and blue). Officially, the red symbolizes Namibia's most valuable resource: its people, and their heroic determination to build a better future. The white fimbriation symbolizes peace and unity; the green triangle denotes agriculture, while the blue triangle represents Namibia's water resources, the sky, and the Atlantic Ocean. The golden sun signifies life and energy.

NAURU

The coral island of Nauru (also spelled Naoero) has a total area of just 8.2 square miles (21.2 square kilometers). Despite its small scale, its population of around 10,000 people are among the richest in the world, deriving their income from mining high-quality, phosphate rock for use in the manufacture of fertilizer. Unfortunately, the industry has also destroyed the environment that once earned Nauru the name Pleasant Island that the British gave it in 1798. Nearly 80 percent of the island is now uninhabitable, and it is likely that the islanders will have to relocate in the future. Nauru was seized by Germany in 1880, being placed under Australian administration by the League of Nations (and later the United Nations) in 1920. Self-government was achieved in 1966, full independence following in 1968.

The flag of Nauru, which consists of a yellow stripe on a blue field and an off-center, white star, symbolizes the island's geographical position 1° south of the equator in the southwest Pacific Ocean, east of the international dateline. The 12 points of the star are said to represent the island's 12 indigenous tribes.

Formal name:
Republic of Naoero/Republic of Nauru

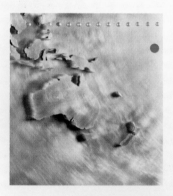

Capital city:
Yaren

Location:
Pacific Ocean

Currency:
1 Australian dollar = 100 cents

Languages:
Nauruan, English

Religions:
Protestant, Roman Catholic

Flag adopted:
January 31, 1968

Flag ratio:
1:2

Formal name:
Sri Nepala Sarkar
(Kingdom of Nepal)

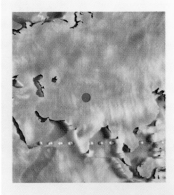

Capital city:
Kathmandu (Katmandu)

Location:
Southern Asia

Currency:
1 Nepalese rupee = 100 paisa

Languages:
Nepali, Indian languages

Religions:
Hindu, Buddhist, Muslim

Flag adopted:
December 16, 1962

Flag ratio:
4:3 (along straight edges)

Situated high in the Himalayas, a number of small Gurkha principalities were united as Nepal under King Prithivi Narayan Shah in 1768. Nepal became a British dependency in 1816, and although its independence was recognized in 1923, it remained bound to Britain by treaty obligations until 1947. It was ruled by a hereditary prime minister from the Rana family from 1845 until 1951, when the family was overthrown in a revolution that restored the monarchy, absolute monarchical control ending only in 1991, when the first multiparty elections were held.

The flag of Nepal is the only national flag that is neither square nor rectangular, instead being based on two, formerly separate, triangular pennants. A crescent moon and part-star motif (the emblem of the royal house) appear on the upper triangle, while a sun motif on the lower triangle symbolizes the Rana family. The combination of the two pennants was said to represent the hope that Nepal would endure for as long as the sun and moon appeared in the sky. Although the sun and moon originally had human faces, these were removed in 1962. The triangles' crimson fields echo the color of Nepal's nation flower, the rhododendron, while the blue border that unites the pennants represents peace.

THE NETHERLANDS

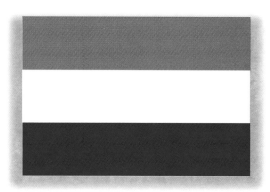

Formal name:
Koninkrijk der Nederlanden
(Kingdom of the Netherlands)

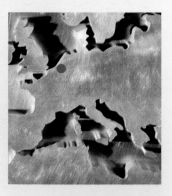

Many Dutch towns, which were generally ruled by merchant groups, became prosperous during the Middle Ages. During the 15th century, the Low Countries (Holland, Belgium, and Flanders) passed to the dukes of Burgundy and to the Spanish Hapsburgs in 1504. Opposition grew to Spanish rule grew, however, and in 1568, led by William, Prince of Orange, the Dutch rebelled against King Philip II of Spain, seven northern provinces forming the United Provinces which was formally recognized as the Dutch Republic in 1648. A struggle between the Orangists, who favored the rule of the *stadholder* (chief magistrate), and republicans ended in 1672, when William of Orange (King William III of England) became *stadholder*, the country becoming a kingdom in 1814.

The Dutch flag, which was possibly the first revolutionary tricolor, may well have been the model for the French *Tricolore*. The first Dutch tricolor, the *Prinsinvlag* ("prince's flag"), of orange, white, and blue, was based on the Prince of Orange's livery. Having proved unstable, by 1660 the orange dye had been changed to red. Until 1800, the order and number of the flag's stripes often varied, and it was not until 1937 that the colors and arrangement were officially established. Every June in the Netherlands, graduating students fly the flag with a school bag on top of the flagpole!

Capital:
The Hague *(political)*
Amsterdam *(economic)*

Location:
Western Europe

Currency:
euro, 1 guilder = 100 cents

Languages:
Dutch, Frysian

Religions:
Roman Catholic, Protestant

Flag adopted:
February 19, 1937

Flag ratio:
2:3

Formal name:
Aotearoa
(New Zealand)

Capital city:
Wellington

Location:
Pacific Ocean

Currency:
1 New Zealand dollar
= 100 cents

Languages:
English, Maori

Religions:
Anglican, Presbyterian, Roman
Catholic

Flag adopted:
June 12, 1902

Flag ratio:
1:2

New Zealand was occupied by the Polynesian Maori people some time before the 15th century, and although the Dutch explorer Abel Tasman reached the two Pacific islands that comprise the country in 1642, the Maori would not let him come ashore. Further exploration of the coast was undertaken by Britain's Captain James Cook from 1769 to 1777, British missionaries beginning to arrive from 1815. The Treaty of Waitangi (1840) between Britain and the Maori having led to British sovereignty over, and colonization of, New Zealand, the colony achieved self-government in 1853. Resenting the loss of their lands, however, the Maori rose in revolt between 1845 and 1847, and again between 1860 and 1872, until they won parliamentary representation. New Zealand was granted dominion status in 1907, achieving full independence from Britain in 1947.

New Zealand's recent history as a British colony is reflected in its flag, which has a British Union Jack in the canton. On the fly, set against a blue field, are four white-fimbriated, red stars of different sizes that together form a stylized representation of the Southern Cross constellation (in fact, only four of the stars in the constellation are depicted: Acrux, Mimosa, Gacrux, and Delta Crucis). Although this flag was designed in 1869, it was restricted to use only at sea until 1902, when it was adopted as the official national flag.

NICARAGUA

Formal name:
República de Nicaragua
(Republic of Nicaragua)

Although Christopher Columbus sighted Nicaragua in 1502, the first European to land on its shores was Gil Gonzalez de Avila, who claimed it for Spain in 1522. It remained a Spanish possession until 1821, when it joined Costa Rica, El Salvador, Honduras, and Guatemala to form the United Provinces of Central America (1823–1838).

While it was a member of this union, Nicaragua adopted the blue-and-white-striped flag of the United Provinces, with its central, triangular emblem, and of all of the national flags of the five former member states, Nicaragua's remains the closest in design to the United Province's flag. The triangular emblem, which symbolizes equality, contains five volcanoes (one for each member state), a rainbow denoting peace and a bright future, and a red, Phrygian cap of liberty, from which sunrays radiate, signifying freedom, all of which appeared on the original emblem. Today, however, the coat of arms displays the name of the national state, *República de Nicaragua,* along with *America Central,* rather than the words *Provincias Unidad del Centro America* ("United Provinces of Central America") that were used in 1823. Nicaragua's original coat of arms, which was very similar to the arms on El Salvador's current flag, was adopted in 1823, but underwent several changes over the years before the current version was introduced in 1971.

Capital city:
Managua

Location:
Central America

Currency:
1 córdoba oro = 100 centavos

Language:
Spanish

Religion:
Roman Catholic

Flag adopted:
August 27, 1971

Flag ratio:
3:5

Formal name:
République du Niger
(Republic of Niger)

Capital city:
Niamey

Location:
West Africa

Currency:
1 C.F.A. franc = 100 centimes

Languages:
French, Hausa, Djerma

Religions:
Sunni Muslim, Animist

Flag adopted:
November 23, 1959

Flag ratio:
2:3

The West African region known as Niger was dominated from the 15th century by the Hausa kingdom and then the Nigerian empire of Sokoto. Explorers arrived on its shores during the 18th century, and the land was also invaded from the north by the Tuareg people. Although the French made it part of French West Africa in 1901, much of the country did not come under French control until 1920. Self-government was achieved in 1920, full independence following in 1960.

Like many of France's former African colonies, Niger's flag is based on the French *Tricolore* and was designed with that of Côte d'Ivoire (Ivory Coast), with whom Niger was allied (along with Chad and Dahomey, now modern Benin), in 1958. Although the flag was adopted in 1959, the anticipated alliance did not occur. Nevertheless, after Niger gained its independence, it continued to use the flag. The orange color symbolizes the Sahara Desert that borders Niger to the north; the green represents the grassy plains of the south and west, as well as the River Niger that waters them; the white denotes hope, as well as the Sahel region of central Niger; while the orange disk in the center of the flag represents the sun shining down on the country.

NIGERIA

Formal name:
Federal Republic of Nigeria

Between the 11th and 14th centuries, the Kanem Empire flourished in northern Nigeria, during which time Islam was introduced. From the 15th century onward, various powerful kingdoms – the Hausa, Yoruba, Benin, and Ibo – emerged, while Portuguese and British slave-traders raided the coast. At the beginning of the 19th century, British exploration of the interior of the country began, the city of Lagos supposedly being purchased from a chief in 1861. In 1914, the two British protectorates of North and South Nigeria were united to form Nigeria, Britain's largest African colony. Nigeria became a federation in 1954, achieving full independence as a constitutional monarchy in 1960 before becoming a republic in 1963.

The national flag that was adopted at independence was Michael Taiwo Akinkunmi's winning design, which was selected from over 2,500 entries submitted to a competition. Although the original design included a red sun with radiating rays and a red stripe, these were removed by the judges to create the current green-and-white flag. The green panels represent agriculture, while the white band denotes the peace between, and unity of, the diverse ethnic peoples of Nigeria, as well as the River Niger, which flows through the country and, as indicated on the flag, irrigates its green fields.

Capital city:
Abuja

Location:
West Africa

Currency:
1 naira = 100 kobo

Languages:
English, Ibo, Yoruba, Hausa

Religions:
Christian, Muslim, Animist

Flag adopted:
October 1, 1960

Flag ratio:
1:2

Formal name:

Kuzey Kibris Turk Cumhuriyeti
(Turkish Republic of Northern
Cyprus)

DISPUTED FLAG

In 1974, Turkish forces invaded Northern Cyprus, effectively partitioning the island of Cyprus. Since this time, United Nations' forces have manned the Attila Line between the Greek south and Turkish north. The self-proclaimed Turkish Republic of Northern Cyprus is not recognized by any nation (apart from Turkey) or the United Nations.

The flag of the Republic of Cyprus (see page 71), which is officially the flag of the whole island, is the only Cypriot flag recognized internationally.

NORTH KOREA

Formal name:
Choson-minjujuui-inmin-konghwaguk
(Democratic People's Republic of Korea)

Although the foundation of the Korean state traditionally dates back to the Tangun Dynasty, in around 2400 B.C., it was not until the 10th century A.D., following centuries of internal wars and invasions, that Korea (North and South) was unified. At the end of World War II, the occupying forces at the time of the ceasefire – Soviet troops north of the 38th Parallel and U.S. troops south of it – created a lasting division of the country into the communist-controlled North Korea and the democratic South Korea.

The North Korean flag was adopted in 1948, when the country became a people's republic under the leadership of the Korean Worker's party (K.W.P.). The traditional colors of the Korean flag – red, white, and blue – were retained, albeit with more emphasis being placed on the symbolism of the red and the addition of a white disk containing a red star. The blue stripes are said to stand for the Korean people's desire for peace, while the red color signifies their revolutionary spirit, the white representing the purity of their ideals. The positioning of the five-pointed star (indicating the nation's path to socialism) on the white disk is reminiscent of the traditional Korean symbol of the universe, the *t'aeguk* (the yin-and-yang symbol).

Capital city:
Pyongyang

Location:
Northeast Asia

Currency:
I won = 100 chon

Languages:
Korean, some Chinese spoken

Religion:
Ch'ondogyo ("Religion of the Heavenly Way," combining elements of Confucianism and Taoism), Buddhist

Flag adopted:
September 8, 1948

Flag ratio:
1:2

Formal name:
Kongeriket Norge
(Kingdom of Norway)

Capital city:
Oslo

Location:
Northwestern Europe

Currency:
1 Norwegian krone = 100 øre

Languages:
Norwegian, Lapp, Finnish

Religion:
Lutheran

Flag adopted:
July 13, 1821

Flag ratio:
8:11

Norway was originally inhabited by the Sammi (Lapp) people, as well as other nomads, being ruled by local chieftains until it was united under King Olaf II in 1015. In 1380, Norway and Denmark were united through royal marriage, Sweden joining Norway and Denmark in the Kalmar Union, under one sovereign, in 1397. Although Sweden broke away from the union in 1523, Norway remained under Danish rule until 1814, when it was ceded to Sweden. Conflict between the Norwegian parliament and the Swedish crown prevailed until 1905, however, when Norway was declared independent and Prince Carl (of Denmark) was elected its king, taking the name Haakon VII.

During the period of Danish rule, Norway flew the *Dannebrog* ("Danish Cloth") until 1814, thereafter briefly flying the Danish flag to which a Norwegian lion had been added. The current flag, the design of Frederik Meltzer, a politician from Bergen, dates from 1821, when a blue Scandinavian cross (representing Sweden, which ruled Norway at that time) was added to the red and white Danish flag. Not only does the flag reflect Norway's historical and continuing links with Denmark and Sweden, but the red, white, and blue colors are also associated with liberty, appearing in the flags of France, the Netherlands, the U.K., and the United States.

OMAN

Formal name:
Saltanaat al-'Umman
(Sultanate of Oman)

Persia ruled Oman from the 4th century A.D. until the 7th century, when Arab armies invaded. The area's flourishing trade with the east attracted the Portuguese in 1507, who founded Muscat and occupied the coast until 1658. Following the Persian reconquest of Oman between 1658 and 1744, in 1749 Ahmad ibn Sa'id became Oman's imam (leader), founding the dynasty that endures to this day. A British presence was established in the area during the late 19th century, Oman not regaining complete independence until 1951, when it became the Sultanate of Muscat and Oman.

Throughout much of this time, Oman used the plain, red banner of the Kharijite Muslims as its flag. In 1970, however, following a bloodless coup, the country was renamed the Sultanate of Oman and a new national flag was adopted. Although red, symbolizing the Omani battles against foreign invaders, continues to be the dominant color, bands of white and green were added to the fly, the white denoting peace and prosperity, and the green the verdant land. In the canton is the sultanate's emblem of two crossed swords superimposed with a *khanjar* (curved dagger) and belt. The flag's proportions were changed from 2:3 to 1:2 in 1995, the vertical hoist stripe also being reduced from one-third to one-quarter of the fly.

Capital city:
Masqat (Muscat)

Location:
Southwest Asia

Currency:
1 Omani rial = 1000 baizas

Languages:
Arabic, Baluchi, English

Religion:
Muslim

Flag adopted:
October 18, 1995

Flag ratio:
1:2

Formal name:
Islamic Republic of Pakistan

Capital city:
Islamabad

Location:
Southern Asia

Currency:
1 Pakistan rupee = 100 paisa

Languages:
Urdu, Punjabi

Religion:
Sunni Muslim

Flag adopted:
August 14, 1947

Flag ratio:
2:3

From the 18th century, Pakistan was ruled as part of British India, being divided into two dominions, India and Pakistan, in 1947, fear of domination by the Hindu majority in India having led to the formation of the separate Muslim state of Pakistan. Pakistan's name, which was devised in 1930 by Choudrat Rahmat Ali for a Muslim division of British India, was derived from the names of the Muslim parts of the Indian Subcontinent: Punjab, the Afghan N.W. Frontier, Kashmir, Sind, and Baluchistan. In Urdu, *Pak* furthermore means "pure," while *stan* means "land."

The Pakistani flag is based on the flag of the All-India Muslim League, which was founded in 1906 by the Aga Khan. Originally green, with a central white star and crescent, a white stripe at the hoist was added to represent non-Muslim minority groups in Pakistan, the predominant dark-green color representing the Muslim majority. Although the crescent is an Islamic emblem, it also symbolizes progress, while the five-pointed star signifies light and knowledge. Legend attributes the design of the flag to Muhammed Ali-Jinah, the founder of the Pakistani nation and president of the Muslim League, but Ameer-ud-din Khidwai is officially credited as the designer.

PALAU

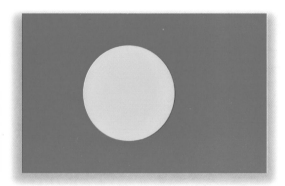

Formal name:
Belu'u era Belau
(Republic of Palau)

Spain governed this island group in the Pacific Ocean from 1600 before selling it to Germany in 1899. Although Japan made it its Micronesian headquarters during World War II, in 1947 Palau became part of the Trust Territory of the Pacific Islands which was established by the United Nations and administered by the United States.

The flag of the trust territory was a blue field bearing six stars arranged in a hexagon to represent its members (Palau, the Marshall Islands, Kosrae, Pohnpei, Truk, and Yap). Palau gained self-government in 1980, officially adopting its flag of blue and yellow in the following year, when it became a republic. (Full independence from trust-territory status, in free association with the United States (which manages the country's defense), and membership of the United Nations was effected in 1994.) Although a very simple design, the symbolism of the Palauan flag is complex. Like many other nations in the region, the blue of Palau's flag indicates its location in the Pacific Ocean, but also symbolizes the islands' transition from territory to republic. The golden disk, set slightly toward the hoist, represents the full moon, which, in Palauan tradition, denotes a time for celebration, as well as being a symbol of peace.

Capital city:
Koror

Location:
Pacific Ocean

Currency:
1 U.S. dollar = 100 cents

Languages:
Palauan, English

Religion:
Roman Catholic

Flag adopted:
January 1, 1981

Flag ratio:
5:8

Formal name:
Al-Solata al-Wataniya Al-Filastiniya
(Palestinian National Authority)

DISPUTED FLAG

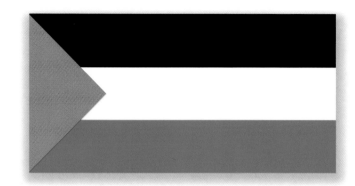

Capital city:
Gaza City (provisional)

Location:
Western Asia, in areas occupied
by Israel and Jordan

Currency:
Israeli shekel, Jordanian dinar

Languages:
Arabic, Hebrew

Religions:
Muslim, Jewish, Christian

The Palestinian Authority and Israel are in continuing negotiation over the final settlement of Palestine. Negotiations include the status of the disputed territory of East Jerusalem (which is claimed by both sides) and of other sites sacred to both Muslims and Jews.

The Palestinian flag is similar to the Jordanian flag (see page 112), but without Jordan's star emblem. Designed as the flag of Arab Revolt in 1916, it was subsequently adopted by the Palestinian Liberation Organization (P.L.O.), which was established in 1964. This flag was internationally recognized in 1974, when the P.L.O. was granted United Nations' Observer Status.

PANAMA

Panama was visited by Christopher Columbus in 1501, Vasco Núñez de Balboa discovering the route from the Atlantic to the Pacific oceans from the Darien Isthmus in 1513. Having been governed by Spain as part of New Granada, Panama gained its independence in 1821. It then became part of Gran Colombia and remained a province until 1903, when, with help from the United States, it became an independent nation, the U.S. simultaneously acquiring the rights to build the Panama Canal.

The flag that was originally proposed for Panama in 1903 consisted of seven red and yellow stripes and a blue canton charged with two golden suns symbolizing the linking of the Atlantic and Pacific oceans by the Panama Canal. This design was rejected by the country's president, Manuel Amador Guerrero, whose replacement flag was loosely modeled on the U.S.'s "Stars and Stripes." The prototype having been sewn by his wife, the rectangular flag is divided into four quarters of red (one), white (two), and blue (one). The colors signify the two main political parties, the liberals (red) and the conservatives (blue), while the white denotes the hoped-for peace between them. The blue star in one white quarter represents the honesty of the country's life, while the red star in the other symbolizes the law and authority of the republic.

Formal name:
República de Panamá
(Republic of Panama)

Capital city:
Panamá (Panama City)

Location:
Central America

Currency:
1 balboa = 100 centesimos

Language:
Spanish

Religions:
Roman Catholic, Protestant, Muslim

Flag adopted:
December 20, 1903

Flag ratio:
2:3

PAPUA NEW GUINEA

Formal name:
Papua Niugini
(Independent State of Papua
New Guinea)

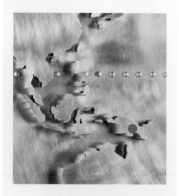

Capital city:
Port Moresby

Location:
Australasia

Currency:
I kina = 100 toea

Languages:
English, some 700 Papuan
languages and dialects

Religions:
Animist, Protestant, Roman
Catholic

Flag adopted:
July 1, 1971

Flag ratio:
3:4

New Guinea has been inhabited for at least 50,000 years, and was probably first settled by peoples from the eastern Indonesian islands. The first European visitor, in about 1526, was the Portuguese explorer Jorge de Menezes, who named it *Ilhas dos Papua* ("The Island of Papua"). The Spanish claimed the island during the mid-16th century, naming it New Guinea because they believed that the inhabitants resembled those of the coastal regions of Guinea, Africa. The Dutch gained control of the western half of the island (New Guinea) in 1828, Britain claiming the southeastern part (Territory of Papua) in 1884, and Germany the northeastern part (Territory of New Guinea). The territories of Papua and New Guinea were united in 1946, when they were made a United Nations' trust territory administered by Australia, before gaining independence as Papua New Guinea in 1975. (The Netherlands ceded the western part of the island in 1962, which is now the Indonesian province of Irian Jaya).

The current flag, which was adopted in 1971, was designed by Susan Karike, a local art teacher, in traditional colors. A golden *kumul* (bird of paradise) flies across the upper red triangle, symbolizing Papua New Guinea's emergence into nationhood. The five white stars in the lower black triangle represent the Southern Cross constellation and symbolize both the country's location and its links with other Pacific nations.

PARAGUAY

Formal name:
República del Paraguay
(Republic of Paraguay)

Originally inhabited by the Guarani people, Paraguay was first reached by Europeans during the 1520s, Jesuit missionaries later administering the country from 1600 until their expulsion in 1767. It then became part of the Spanish Viceroyalty of Peru and, from 1776, part of the Viceroyalty of Buenos Aires, before declaring its independence from Spain in 1811.

Influenced by the French *Tricolore*, which had become a symbol of liberation, a number of variant designs of the Paraguayan flag were in use prior to the adoption of the current flag in 1842. Red, white, and blue flags were carried by Paraguayan troops defending Buenos Aires against British invasion in 1806, for example, while in 1814, during the regime of José de Francia, a tricolor was flown that bore the arms of the city of Asunción on one side and those of the king of Spain on the other. The current flag continues the unusual practice of featuring emblems on each side: on the obverse (front) is the country's name and the "Star of May," indicating the month in which Paraguay gained its independence; on the reverse is the "Treasury Seal" of Paraguay, which depicts a lion guarding a pole supporting a cap of liberty. The motto reads *Paz y Justicia* ("Peace and Justice").

Capital city:
Asunción

Location:
South America

Currency:
1 Paraguayan guarani
= 100 céntimos

Languages:
Spanish, Guarani

Religion:
Roman Catholic

Flag adopted:
November 25, 1842

Flag ratio:
3:5

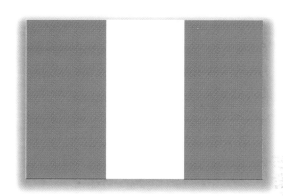

Formal name:
República del Perú
(Republic of Peru)

Capital city:
Lima

Location:
South America

Currency:
1 neuvo sol = 100 centimos

Languages:
Spanish, Quechua, Aymara

Religion:
Roman Catholic

Flag adopted:
February 25, 1825

Flag ratio:
2:3

The Chimu culture flourished in Peru from around 1200 A.D., but was gradually superseded by the Inca Empire. On his arrival in Peru in 1531, the Spanish conquistador Francisco Pizzaro began looting its riches and enslaving its people. By 1533, when the last Inca emperor, Atahaulpa, was assassinated, Spanish rule was firmly established, Lima subsequently serving as the administrative center of the Viceroyalty of Peru. A revolt against Spanish rule by the Tupac Amaru in 1780 having failed, Peru remained the last Spanish dominion, as well as the last to achieve independence, which it attained in 1824.

The red and white colors of the Peruvian flag, which are said to be those of the Inca Empire, were chosen by General José de San Martín, who played an important role in liberating Chile and Argentina from Spanish rule before leading his army of independence in Peru in 1820. Legend tells that San Martín saw a flock of flamingos with white breasts and red wings flying over his troops; interpreting them as a good omen, their colors were declared those of liberty. Peru's red-and-white flag was originally charged with another Inca emblem, a rising sun, which was dropped at the request of Simón Bolívar in 1825, when the flag assumed its present form.

PHILIPPINES

In 1521, Ferdinand Magellan became the first European to sight the Philippines, which he named after the king of Spain, Philip II. With Spanish rule having spread during the 16th century, during the 19th century strengthening nationalism and resentment against economic injustices led to a series of armed revolts. In 1898, during the Spanish-American War, the United States sank the Spanish fleet in Manila Bay and the Philippines declared its independence, subsequently, however, being ceded to the U.S. Armed resistance to foreign rule continued until 1935, when internal self-rule was granted, the Philippines becoming an independent republic in 1946.

The national flag of the Philippines has its origins in the liberation movement of the 1890s: designed by General Aguinaldo in 1897, it was carried into battle against the Spanish in May 1898. The eight-rayed sun (for the eight provinces that rose in revolt) and three golden stars (representing the major regions of Luzon, the Visayas, and Mindanao) on the white triangle symbolize the dawn of a new era. The red stripe represents courage, while the blue stripe denotes patriotism (during times of war, the order of the stripes is reversed). The white triangle signifies both peace and the Katipunan, the revolutionary organization that led the fight for independence.

Formal name:
Republika ng Pilipinas
(Republic of the Philippines)

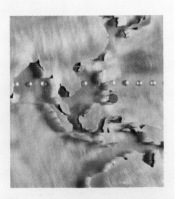

Capital city:
Manila

Location:
Southeast Asia

Currency:
1 Philippine peso
= 100 centavos

Languages:
Tagalog (Filipino) English,
Spanish

Religions:
Roman Catholic, Muslim

Flag adopted:
May 19, 1898

Flag ratio:
1:2

Formal name:
Rzeczpospolita Polska
(Republic of Poland)

Capital city:
Warszawa (Warsaw)

Location:
Northern Europe

Currency:
1 zloty = 100 groszy

Language:
Polish

Religion:
Roman Catholic

Flag adopted:
August 1, 1919

Flag ratio:
5:8

The Polish tribes were first united under a Christian ruler, Mieczyslaw, during the 10th century. By the end of the 14th century, Poland was both a great power and, having united with Lithuania, the largest country in Europe. Wars with Russia, Sweden, and Brandenburg during the mid-17th century, as well as the Ottoman Empire during the 18th, laid the country open to interference from Austria, Prussia, and Russia, however, culminating in their occupation of Poland in 1795. Although uprisings in 1830, 1848, and 1863 led to greater repression by Russia, taking advantage of the internal crisis in Russia following the Bolshevik Revolution, in 1919 Poland declared itself an independent republic. Its strategic position in Northern Europe has meant that Poland has suffered occupation and annexation throughout the 20th century, its shifting borders not being permanently fixed until 1945.

The colors of the Polish flag have their origin in medieval pennants, a red flag with a white eagle being used by King Wladyslaw Jagiello at the Battle of Grunwald in 1410. The colors were again used during the 1830 uprising in the form of red-and-white ribbons worn by patriots, and they were officially recognized as the national colors in 1919.

PORTUGAL

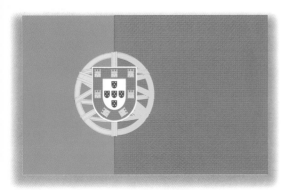

Formal name:
República Portugusea
(Republic of Portugal)

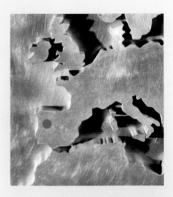

In 1139, Portugal became an independent monarchy under King Alfonso Henriques, who, in 1147, captured Lisbon from the Moors, who were expelled from Portugal during the following century. By the 15th century, Portugal had grown into a dynamic trading nation which, encouraged by Prince Henry the Navigator, played a leading role in sea exploration beyond Europe's shores, so that by the mid-16th century, Portugal claimed a vast empire in Brazil, Africa, and Asia. Crippled by civil war from 1832 to 1834, however, Portugal's political instability continued throughout the 19th century.

The monarchy having been overthrown in 1910, with the declaration of the new Republic of Portugal came a new flag. The field of red and green, chosen to symbolize both revolution (red) and Portugal's tradition of exploration (green, for "new lands"), was charged with an emblem that symbolizes Portugal's imperial past: a shield superimposed on a gold armillary sphere (an early navigational device). The central white shield charged with five blue shields represents Alfonso Henriques's victory over five Moorish princes in 1139, their white markings denoting the five wounds of Christ, while the seven gold castles in the red orle (the shield's border) signify Portugal's expansion as a result of Alfonso Henriques's marriage in 1146.

Capital city:
Lisboa (Lisbon)

Location:
Western Europe

Currency:
1 escudo = 100 centavos

Language:
Portuguese

Religion:
Roman Catholic

Flag adopted:
June 30, 1911

Flag ratio:
2:3

Formal name:
Dawlat al'Qatar
(State of Qatar)

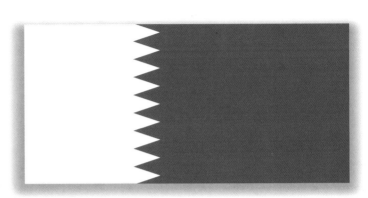

Capital city:
Al Dawdah (Doha)

Location:
Southwest Asia

Currency:
1 riyal = 100 dihrams

Languages:
Arabic, English

Religion:
Muslim

Flag adopted:
July 9, 1971

Flag ratio:
11:28

Qatar used to be under the control of Bahrain and consequently used the same plain red flag of the Khajirite Muslims until around 1860. Following a British request, all of the countries in the region added white to their flags (by adding a white stripe to the hoist) to distinguish them from those of pirates. When, in 1916, the British government formally recognized Sheikh Abdullah al-Thani as Qatar's ruler, Qatar adopted a white flag with a red square in the center and a red crescent in the canton. It later returned to a red field with a serrated white stripe.

In around 1932, the flag's proportions were changed to 1:2, the serration was changed to a wavy stripe, and the red became darker. In 1936, the ratio was again altered – to 11:30 – the red being changed to maroon, with nine (serrated points and ten red diamonds in the serration. In 1949, yet more changes were made, the current color, known as "Qatar maroon," being adopted, the serration being extended to a point one-third across the flag, and the diamonds being removed. In 1971, when Qatar became fully independent, a nearly identical flag to the 1949 version was adopted, the only thing that was changed was the ratio, which was now set at 11:28.

ROMANIA

Formal name:
România
(Romania)

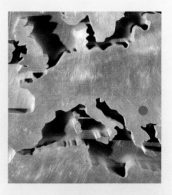

Capital city:
Bucuresti (Bucharest)

Location:
Southeastern Europe

Currency:
1 Romanian leu = 100 bani

Languages:
Romanian, Hungarian

Religions:
Romanian Orthodox, Roman
Catholic

Flag adopted:
December 27, 1989

Flag ratio:
2:3

Romania was once the Roman province of Dacia, being later overrun by the Goths, Huns, Bulgars, and Slavs before falling to the Ottoman Empire during the 15th century. Turkish rule having been replaced by Russian protection from 1829 to 1856, in 1859, Moldavia (in the south) and Wallachia (in the east) elected Prince Alexander Cuza as their ruler, the unified country being recognized internationally as being independent in 1878. In 1946, however, a communist coalition government forced the monarch's abdication and proclaimed the Romanian People's Republic. Following more than forty years of strict communist rule, the oppressive regime of Nicolae Ceausescu was overturned in 1989, whereupon free elections were held.

The Romanian flag dates from 1848, the year of revolutions throughout Europe, when, encouraged by the French example, and in common with many other emerging nations, Romania adopted a tricolor banner. The Romanian colors of blue, yellow, and red, which date back to the banners of the former Roman province and were retained even after the advent of communism, also represent the provinces of Wallachia (blue and yellow) and Moldavia (red and blue). From 1866 to 1948, the tricolor carried the royal arms in the middle of the yellow stripe, these being replaced by the communist emblem in 1948, which was in turn removed following Ceausescu's fall in 1989.

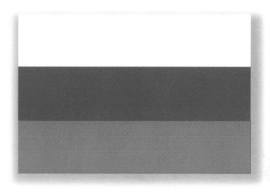

Formal name:
Rossiyskaya Federatsiya
(Russian Federation)

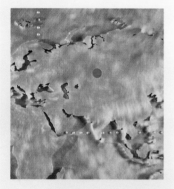

Capital city:
Moskva (Moscow)

Location:
Eurasia

Currency:
1 rouble = 100 kopecks

Language:
Russian

Religions:
Russian Orthodox, Muslim

Flag adopted:
August 22, 1991

Flag ratio:
2:3

The world's largest country in terms of area, Russia was once the biggest, and most powerful, of all of the Soviet socialist republics that made up the Union of Soviet Socialist Republics (U.S.S.R.). Russia became an independent country in 1991, when the U.S.S.R. was dissolved. Administratively, Russia includes twenty-one republics (each with their own flag), six *krays* (territories), ten *okrugs* (national areas), forty-nine *oblasts* (regions), one autonomous *oblast*, and two cities with federal status.

It is said that Czar Peter the Great adopted a form of the Dutch flag during an incognito visit to the Netherlands in 1697, albeit rearranging the order of the colors to create the Russian flag. The white band is said to represent God, the blue band the czar, and the red band the people, the blue stripe of the czar being below God, but above the people. Another interpretation is that these were originally the colors of Moscow. Since the 19th century, the colors have been used by many Eastern European nations and have become known as the Pan-Slavic colors. Following the Russian Revolution of 1917, the communist regime abolished all former flags, replacing them the "Red Flag" of the Soviet Union. When it became independent in 1991, however, Russia readopted its traditional tricolor.

RWANDA

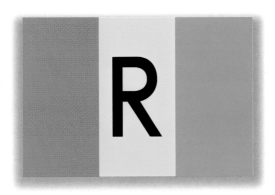

Formal name:
Republika y'u Rwanda
(Republic of Rwanda)

Composed of two main ethnic groups, the Hutu and Tutsi, along with the Twa pygmies, the feudal kingdom of Rwanda was linked within the empire of East German Africa to neighboring Urundi (now Burundi) from 1819 to 1919. It was subsequently governed by Belgium under a League of Nations' mandate, before becoming a United Nations' trust territory. In 1961, the monarchy (representing the dominant, yet minority, Tutsi people) was overthrown by the Hutus, and Ruanda, as it was then called, achieved full independence in 1962.

When the republic was proclaimed in June 1961, the Pan-African colors that symbolize African nationalism and unity were planned for Rwanda's flag in the form of three vertical stripes arranged in the order green (hoist), yellow (middle), and red (fly). Just three months earlier, on March 21, 1961, however, Mali had adopted an identical flag, so the order of the Rwandan colors changed to red (hoist), yellow (middle), and green (fly). It was soon recognized that this version was identical to the flag of Guinea, and an "R" was added prior to Independence Day, July 1, 1962, to signify "R(wanda) born through R(evolution) and confirmed by R(eferendum)."

Note On September 30, 1999, the Rwandan government proposed replacing the current flag, which it feels has too strong an association with the genocide of 1994. To date, however, a new design has not been agreed.

Capital city:
Kigali

Location:
Central Africa

Currency:
1 Rwanda franc = 100 centimes

Languages:
French, Kinyarwanda, Swahili

Religions:
Animist, Roman Catholic

Flag adopted:
September 1961, altered 1962

Flag ratio:
2:3

ST. CHRISTOPHER AND NEVIS

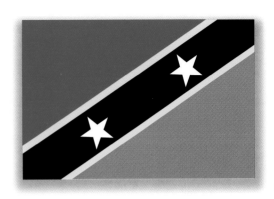

Formal name:
Federation of St. Christopher (St. Kitts) and Nevis; also known as St. Kitts and Nevis

Capital city:
Basseterre

Location:
Caribbean

Currency:
1 East Caribbean dollar
= 100 cents

Language:
English, local dialects

Religion:
Protestant, Roman Catholic

Flag adopted:
September 19, 1983

Flag ratio:
2:3

The islands of St. Christopher and Nevis, in the Caribbean's Leeward Islands, were named by Christopher Columbus in 1493, St. Kitts, as St. Christopher is more usually known, being named in honor of his patron saint. In 1623, St. Kitts became Britain's first West Indian colony, Nevis being settled soon thereafter. Although the French seized the islands on several occasions, St. Kitts, Nevis, and the neighboring Anguilla were united as a British dependency in 1871. The islands gained self-government as the West Indies Associated States in 1967, and although it withdrew from the association in 1980, Anguilla remained a British dependency, while St. Kitts and Nevis jointly attained full independence in 1983.

The flag that was adopted to represent St. Kitts and Nevis was the result of a competition and was designed by a student, Edrice Lewis. Like those of many other Caribbean nations, the flag incorporates the Pan-African colors of green, red, and yellow, although the official interpretation of the flag attributes a more specific symbolism to the colors. The green is said to represent the islands' fertile land, the red their struggle for freedom, and the yellow the sunshine that is enjoyed by the islands throughout the year. The African heritage of many of the islands' people is symbolized by the black diagonal, the two stars signifying hope and liberty.

ST. LUCIA

Formal name:
St. Lucia

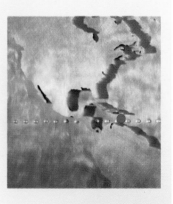

Although St. Lucia was discovered by Christopher Columbus in 1502, the first colonists were the French, who signed a treaty with the indigenous Carib people in 1660 and began settling on the island in 1635. From 1663, sovereignty of the island passed between France and Britain several times before it was finally ceded to Britain in 1803. A British colony within the federal system of the Windward Islands until 1960, St. Lucia gained self-government within the federation in 1967. The associated states having agreed to seek independence separately in 1975, St. Lucia achieved this goal in 1979.

During the period of French rule, the island had flown the same flag as its island neighbor, Martinique. On the achievement of self-government in 1967, St. Lucia adopted a flag designed by a local artist, Dunstan St. Omer. The flag represents the island surrounded by the blue waters of the Caribbean and Atlantic Ocean, the two triangular shapes representing two volcanoes, the Pitons, the yellow triangle symbolizing the Caribbean sunshine, and the black arrowhead fimbriated with white signifying the harmony of the dual racial culture of St. Lucia. From 1967, when St. Lucia became an associated British state, to 1979, when it became independent, the height of the golden triangle was lower, and the blue field a lighter shade, than in today's flag.

Capital city:
Castries

Location:
Caribbean

Currency:
1 East Caribbean dollar
= 100 cents

Languages:
English, French, local dialects

Religion:
Roman Catholic

Flag adopted:
February 22, 1979

Flag ratio:
1:2

ST. VINCENT AND THE GRENADINES

Formal name:
St. Vincent and the Grenadines

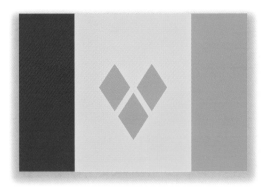

Capital city:
Kingstown

Location:
Caribbean

Currency:
1 East Caribbean dollar
= 100 cents

Language:
English

Religions:
Protestant, Roman Catholic

Flag adopted:
October 21, 1985

Flag ratio:
2:3

Despite Christopher Columbus having landed on St. Vincent in 1498, the islands were fiercely defended by Carib people, not being successfully colonized (by the British) until 1762. The island of St. Vincent itself, along with the northern islands of the Grenadines group (the largest of which are Bequia, Canouan, Mustique, Mayreau, and Union) were part of the West Indies Federation until 1962. They acquired self-government as an associated state of Britain in 1969, full independence being gained in October 1979.

The flag that was first hoisted at independence was the result of a national competition and contained a stylized breadfruit leaf in the center, on which the islands' arms were placed. The design did not meet with universal approval, however, since the breadfruit, which was introduced to the Caribbean by the British, was an unwelcome reminder of the colonial past, so a new flag was commissioned in 1985. Called "The Gems," the colors of the flag symbolize the blue of the sky and sea, the lush, green vegetation, and the bright, "golden" spirit of the people. In place of the arms, a "V" shape made up of three green diamonds was used to represent St. Vincent and the Grenadines, reflecting the local saying that the islands are the "gems of the Antilles."

SAMOA

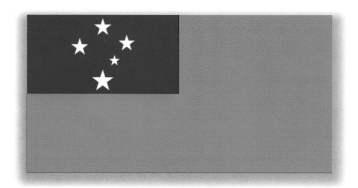

Formal name:
Malo Sa'oloto Tuto'atasi o Samoa
(Independent State of Samoa)

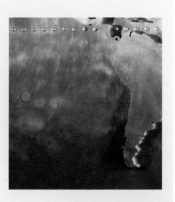

The first Europeans to reach the Pacific island group of Samoa were the Dutch, in 1722. During the 19th century, Germany, Britain, and the United States competed for influence over the islands, resulting in their division, in 1899, into American Samoa and the German colony of Western Samoa, which consisted of the islands of Savai'i, Upolu, Manono, and Apolima. After World War I, Western Samoa was administered by New Zealand, becoming the first independent Polynesian nation in 1962 and changing its official name to Samoa in 1997.

Western Samoa's traditional rulers, the kings of Malietoa and Tamasese, had their own flags: the Malietoa flag had a plain red field, with a white cross and star in the canton, while the Tamasese flag consisted of a black cross on a white field, with a white star in a red canton. As a territory of New Zealand, in 1948 Samoa adopted a flag that was created by combining the red field of the Malietoa flag and the four stars of the Southern Cross constellation that appear on the New Zealand flag, which were placed on a blue field in the canton. Having been modified to include five stars in 1949, this flag was retained when Samoa became independent.

Capital city:
Apia

Location:
Pacific Ocean

Currency:
1 tala = 100 sene

Languages:
Samoan, English

Religions:
Protestant, Roman Catholic

Flag adopted:
January 1, 1962

Flag ratio:
1:2

Formal name:
Repubblica di San Marino
(Republic of San Marino)

Capital city:
San Marino

Location:
Southern Europe

Currency:
1 Italian lira = 100 centesimi

Language:
Italian

Religion:
Roman Catholic

Flag adopted:
April 6, 1862

Flag ratio:
3:4

According to tradition, San Marino, a landlocked enclave in Northern Italy and one of the world's smallest republics, was founded in A.D. 301 by a Christian stonemason called Marinus, who had sought refuge from religious persecution on Mount Tizano. Through both its isolated position in the Eastern Apennines and its ability to treat with its more powerful neighbors, the republic was able to maintain its autonomy, its independence being recognized by Pope Nicholas IV in 1292, by Napoleon in 1797, the Congress of Vienna in 1815, the kingdom of Italy in 1862, and subsequently also the Republic of Italy.

The flag of San Marino dates back to 1797, its colors having been derived from the republic's coat of arms, which consist of a heart-shaped shield topped by a crown. The blue is said to denote the sky over San Marino, while the white represents the clouds above, and the snow upon, Mount Tizano. Within the shield are the three citadel towers of Guaita, Cesta, and Montale, which are situated on the summit of Mount Tizano, symbolizing the republic's ability to defend its freedom. Although the arms do not appear on the national flag, they are used on the state flag that is flown on official occasions.

SÃO TOMÉ AND PRÍNCIPE

Formal name:
República Democrática de São Tomé e Príncipe
(Democratic Republic of São Tomé and Príncipe)

The two islands of São Tomé and Príncipe, off the western coast of Africa, were uninhabited until the arrival of the Portuguese in 1471, who settled the islands with convicts and exiled Jews. Slavery became an important aspect of the islands' trade, forced labor being used to work the sugar and coffee plantations, and, the cacao tree having been introduced to the islands in 1822, São Tomé and Príncipe also becoming a leading producer of cocoa during the 19th century. A colony until 1951, when São Tomé and Príncipe became an overseas province of Portugal, the islands achieved self-government in 1973, full independence following in 1975.

The national flag is based on the flag flown by members of the liberation movement, the *Movimento de Liberacion de São Tomé e Príncipe* (M.L.S.T.P.), although in the M.L.S.T.P.'s flag, all three horizontal stripes were of the same width. The combination of red, yellow, and green stripes with black stars is based on the flag of Ghana (the first independent African nation), whose Pan-African colors have served as the inspiration for many African flags. The two black stars represent the islands of São Tomé and Príncipe, while the red triangle in the hoist symbolizes the struggle for independence.

Capital:
São Tomé

Location:
West Africa

Currency:
1 dobra = 100 centimos

Language:
Portuguese, Fang (Bantu)

Religion:
Roman Catholic

Flag adopted:
November 5, 1975

Flag ratio:
1:2

Formal name:
*Al Mamlakah al Arabiyah as
Sa'udiyah*
(Kingdom of Saudi Arabia)

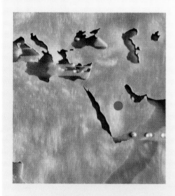

Capital city:
Ar Riyad (Riyadh)

Location:
Southwest Asia

Currency:
1 Saudi riyal = 20 qursh
= 100 halala

Language:
Arabic

Religion:
Muslim

Flag adopted:
March 15, 1973

Flag ratio:
2:3

Modern Saudi Arabia is almost entirely the creation of Abd-al Aziz ibn Saud (1880–1953), the first king of Saudi Arabia, who ruled from 1932 to 1953. From 1918 to 1925 ibn Saud fought rival Arab rulers to establish himself as king of the Hejaz and sultan of Nejd, these territories being united as the Kingdom of Saudi Arabia in 1932.

The green of the Saudi Arabian flag's field is the color of the Prophet Muhammad and was favored by the Wahabi, a puritanical Saudi Islamic sect founded by Muhammad ibn-Abd-al-Wahab (1703–92) that had spread throughout the Arabian Peninsula by the early 20th century and today remains the official religious ideology of Saudi Arabia. The inscription on the flag is the *shahada*, the Muslim statement of faith, which reads, "There is no god but Allah and Muhammad is the prophet of Allah." The *shahada* was added to the flag in 1901 and appears on both of its sides. (Because Arabic script is read from right to left, the *shahada* on the reverse side is manufactured separately as a cutout before being applied to the flag to ensure that the text is always read correctly.) Beneath the inscription is a sword commemorating the victories of ibn Saud; the sword's tip points to the left on the obverse side and to the right on the reverse side.

SENEGAL

Formal name:
République du Sénégal
(Republic of Senegal)

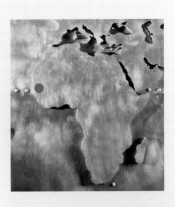

Once part of the mighty medieval empire of Mali, Senegal was explored by the Portuguese during the 15th century before coming under French control from the 17th century. Having had a French governor from 1854, in 1895 Senegal became part of the colony of French West Africa (along with the modern nations of Mauritania, Sudan, Burkina Faso, Guinea, Niger, Côte d'Ivoire, and Benin). Senegal was led to independence in June 1960 by Léopold Sédar Senghor, a poet and the founder of *negritude*, a black literary and philosophical movement.

When preparing for independence, in 1959 Senegal formed the Federation of Mali in association with its neighbor and adopted the federation flag. This was a tricolor of green, yellow, and red vertically arranged stripes (which followed the design of the French *Tricolore* while using the Pan-African colors pioneered by Ghana), charged with a black emblem known as a *kanaga*, a stylized human figure. Following the dissolution of the federation in August 1960, Senegal adopted a new flag. Although the colored stripes were retained, the *kanaga* emblem was replaced by a green star, symbolizing the opening up of Senegal to the five continents. During the period of the Senegambia Confederation (a federation between Senegal and the Gambia), which lasted from 1981 to 1989, neither Senegal nor Gambia altered their national emblems.

Capital city:
Dakar

Location:
West Africa

Currency:
1 C.F.A. franc = 100 centimes

Languages:
French, diverse tribal languages

Religions:
Muslim, Christian, Animist

Flag adopted:
September 1960

Flag ratio:
2:3

SEYCHELLES

Formal name:
Republik Sesel
(Republic of Seychelles)

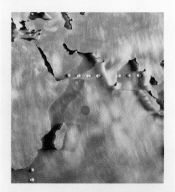

Capital city:
Victoria

Location:
Indian Ocean

Currency:
1 Seychelles rupee = 100 cents

Languages:
Creole, English, French

Religions:
Roman Catholic, Protestant

Flag adopted:
June 18, 1996

Flag ratio:
1:2

Seychelles consists of around 115 islands in the western part of the Indian Ocean, most of which are low-lying, uninhabited, coral islands. The 32 islands of the Mahé group contain the principal islands, including Mahé Island (the largest), Praslin, La Digue, and Silhouette. First visited by European explorers during the early 16th century, Seychelles was claimed and settled by the French in 1756 and then ceded to Britain in 1914, after which it was ruled as part of Mauritius until it became a crown colony in 1903. Seychelles gained full independence in 1976.

The flag that the newly independent Seychelles adopted was a white saltire (a diagonal cross) dividing a field of blue (hoist and fly) and red (top and bottom). Following a coup, in 1977 this flag was replaced with one based on the party flag of the ruling Marxist Seychelles People's United Party (S.P.U.P.), being green, white, and red, with the colors arranged in horizontal, wavy bands. The third, and current, Seychelles flag was formally adopted in 1996 as a nonpartisan flag suited to the new era of multiparty democracy (all of the political parties' colors are included). The oblique bands symbolize the sky and sea (blue), the sun (yellow), the people (red), social harmony and justice (white), and the land (green).

SIERRA LEONE

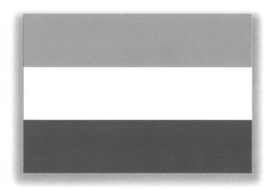

Formal name:
Republic of Sierra Leone

Freetown, the capital of Sierra Leone, which was founded in 1787 by British philanthropists as a home for freed slaves, became a British colony in 1808, the interior lands of Sierra Leone being added to it in 1896.

Until 1961, when Sierra Leone achieved full independence, it flew a British colonial flag with a British Union Jack in the canton, the field being charged with a badge featuring a palm tree against the background of a landscape. This colonial flag was also common to the Gambia and the Gold Coast (now Ghana) when they were British possessions, each country being distinguished by the placement of its initials – "S.L.," "G.," or "G.C." – at the bottom of the badge. On becoming independent in 1961, Sierra Leone adopted a new flag that consisted of a horizontal tricolor of green, white, and blue. The green band represents the country's agriculture, the savannah of Northern Sierra Leone, and the dense forests of the southeast; the white band symbolizes peace and justice; and the blue band denotes the waters of the Atlantic Ocean, on whose shores the harbor of Freetown is located, as well as the numerous rivers that flow through the country.

Capital city:
Freetown

Location:
West Africa

Currency:
1 leone = 100 cents

Languages:
English, Mende, Temne, Krio (Creole)

Religions:
Animist, Muslim, Christian

Flag adopted:
April 27, 1961

Flag ratio:
2:3

Formal name:
Hsin-chia-p'o Kung-ho-kuo/Republik Singapura/Singapore Kudiyarasu
(Republic of Singapore)

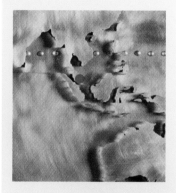

Capital city:
Singapore

Location:
Southeast Asia

Currency:
1 Singapore dollar = 100 cents

Languages:
Chinese, Malay, Tamil, English
(all official languages)

Religions:
Buddhist, Christian, Muslim,
Taoist, Hindu

Flag adopted:
December 3, 1959

Flag ratio:
2:3

Singapore, which comprises one main island (Singapore Island) and fifty adjacent islands, lies between Malaysia (to the north) and Indonesia (to the south). Once a swampy jungle, in 1819 the fortunes of Singapore were vitalized by Sir Thomas Stamford Raffles, of the British East India Company, and it rapidly developed into a major port for shipping tin and rubber. Its strategic importance led it to become a British colony during the 19th century and a vital military base in the Far East. Singapore became self-governing in 1946. Having joined the Federation of Malaysia in 1963, it seceded from it in 1965 and declared itself an independent republic.

Singapore's flag uses the traditional colors of the Malay people: red, symbolizing universal brotherhood and equality, and white, denoting purity and virtue. The white crescent originally served as a symbol to assure the Malays that although its population was three-quarters Chinese, Singapore was not a Chinese state, the crescent moon today being said to represent the birth of the new nation of Singapore. Although the original design featured just three stars, because it was feared that they might imply an association with communism, the number was increased to five to represent Singapore's five ideals: democracy, peace, progress, justice, and equality.

SLOVAKIA

Slovakia was part of Hungary from the 11th century until 1918, when it was united with the Czech lands of Bohemia and Moravia to form Czechoslovakia. In 1938, under pressure from the German dictator Adolf Hitler, Slovakia declared its independence, but instead became a puppet fascist state. Following a popular revolt against German rule, and liberation in 1944, Czechoslovakia was re-established in 1945. In 1993, Slovakia and the Czech Republic separated to become independent states.

The first Slovak flag was a red-and-white bicolor that was initially flown in April 1848 as a sign of Slovakia's demands for freedom from Austro-Hungarian rule. A blue stripe was added in August 1848, and the order of the colors was established in 1868. As Czechoslovakia, a red-and-white flag charged with a blue triangle was used, Slovakia re-adopting the tricolor during World War II, to the center of which a red-and-blue shield, fimbriated with white and containing a white Lorraine cross (an ancient Christian symbol), was added. Officially, the cross, which stands on three stylized hills representing the Tatra, Matra, and Fatra mountains, symbolizes three saints: St. Constantine and St. Method (who were said to have brought the symbol to Slovakia), as well as St. Benedict. The shield was moved nearer to the hoist in 1992.

Formal name:
Slovenská Republika
(Slovak Republic)

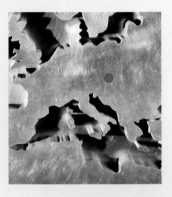

Capital city:
Bratislava

Location:
Eastern Europe

Currency:
Slovak koruna

Languages:
Slovak, Hungarian, Czech

Religions:
Roman Catholic, Protestant

Flag adopted:
September 1, 1992

Flag ratio:
2:3

SLOVENIA

Formal name:
Republika Slovenija
(Republic of Slovenia)

Capital city:
Ljubljana

Location:
Southeastern Europe

Currency:
1 Slovene tolar = 100 stotinov

Language:
Slovene

Religion:
Roman Catholic

Flag adopted:
June 25, 1991

Flag ratio:
1:2

Slovenia was ruled by the Hapsburgs from 1335, subsequently becoming part of the Austro-Hungarian Empire's crownlands of Carniola, Styria, and Carinthia. In 1848, when it was looking to Russia for assistance in gaining independence, Slovenia flew its first Slovenian flag – a tricolor in the Pan-Slavic colors of red, white, and blue – which was immediately banned by the Austrian authorities.

Slovenia was incorporated into the kingdom of the Serbs, Croats, and Slovenes in 1918, which was renamed Yugoslavia in 1929. As part of Yugoslavia, in addition to Yugoslavia's blue-over-white-over-red tricolor (to which Marshal Tito added a gold-fimbriated, red star in 1946), Slovenia flew its own flag, which was distinguished by its white-over-blue-over-red stripes.

Following the collapse of communism in Eastern Europe, Slovenia broke away from Yugoslavia in 1991, its independence being recognized in 1992. Slovenia continued to use the Slovene tricolor, to which a blue shield was added in the canton to create a new national flag. Although the shield is very similar to that featured in Slovakia's flag, the three mountain peaks in the Slovene arms are said to represent Mount Triglav and the Julian Alps. Above the peaks are three golden stars, derived from the ancient arms of the Duchy of Selje, while the two wavy lines beneath the peaks represent Slovenia's Adriatic coastline.

SOLOMON ISLANDS

Formal name:
Solomon Islands

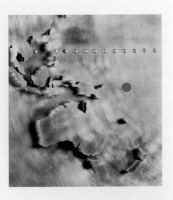

The Solomon Islands are a group of hundreds of atolls and islands that lie in the southwestern waters of the Pacific Ocean. The largest island in the archipelago, as well as the site of the capital city, Honiara, is Guadalcanal. Originally inhabited by Melanesians, the islands were first sighted by European eyes when a expedition from Peru, led by the Spanish navigator Alvaro de Mendaña, discovered them in 1568. The Solomon Islands were colonized by Spain from 1568 to 1606, a period when the islanders were exploited as a source of labor to work on plantations on other Pacific islands. The Solomon Islands became a British protectorate in 1893. During World War II, they were the scene of fierce fighting, including the major battle for Guadalcanal (1942). Self-government was granted in 1976, full independence being achieved in 1978.

The Solomon Islands' national flag was adopted in 1977 in anticipation of independence. Divided diagonally by a yellow stripe, representing the sunshine of the islands, the upper, blue triangle symbolizes the Pacific Ocean, the lower, green triangle signifying the land. The five white stars in the canton initially represented the country's five original provinces, but, following the abolition of the provinces in 1984, the symbolism of the five stars was altered to denote the five main island groups.

Capital city:
Honiara

Location:
Pacific Ocean

Currency:
1 Solomon Island dollar
= 100 cents

Languages:
English, diverse local languages

Religions:
Protestant, Roman Catholic

Flag adopted:
November 18, 1977

Flag ratio:
1:2

Formal name:
*Al Jumhuoriya As-Somalya
Dimocradia*
(Somalia Democratic Republic)

Capital city:
Muqdisho (Mogadishu)

Location:
East Africa

Currency:
I Somali shilling = 100 cents

Languages:
Somali (official), Arabic, English,
Italian

Religion:
Muslim

Flag adopted:
October 12, 1954

Flag ratio:
unspecified, but generally 2:3

Somalia developed around Arab trading posts that grew into sultanates. Its strategic location, on the Horn of Africa, bordering the Indian Ocean, led to European interest in the region, Britain establishing the protectorate of Somaliland in the northern part of the region in 1884, and Italy the protectorate of Somalia in the south in 1889. The Italian region became a colony in 1927, and part of Italian East Africa in 1936, before falling to Britain in 1941. Designated a United Nations' Trust Territory, in 1950 the southern region again returned to Italian administration, although only for a fixed, ten-year term, Somalia becoming a independent republic with the merging of the two former colonies in 1960.

The Somali flag, which was designed by Mohammed Awale Liban in 1954, was based on the blue-and-white flag of the United Nations, which was assisting Somalia along its path toward independence. The blue of the field represents the United Nations, while the white of the star symbolizes peace and prosperity. The star has five points, one for each branch of Somalis who live in different regions: the Somalis of the former Italian Somalia and former British Somaliland, and those living in Ethiopia, Djibouti, and Northern Kenya.

SOMALILAND

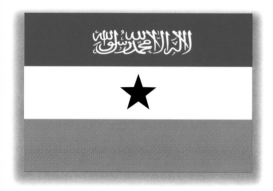

Formal name:
Republic of Somaliland

DISPUTED FLAG

In May 1991, the Republic of Somaliland was proclaimed in the northeastern region of Somalia. Neither the republic nor its flag are recognized by any country or the United Nations, however.

Location:
Northeast Africa

SOUTH AFRICA

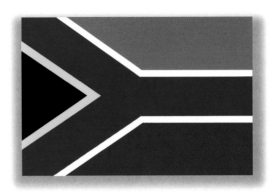

Formal name:
Republic of South Africa

Capital city:
Pretoria *(administrative capital),*
Cape Town *(legislative capital),*
Bloemfontein *(judicial capital)*

Location:
Southern Africa

Currency:
1 rand = 100 cents

Languages:
Afrikaans, English, Xhosa, Zulu

Religions:
Christian denominations,
including Dutch Reformed,
Roman Catholic

Flag adopted:
April 27, 1994

Flag ratio:
2:3

Situated on the southern tip of Africa, South Africa was the home of the Sotho, Swazi, Xhosa, and Zulu peoples before the Dutch East India Company settled Cape Town in 1652. Subsequently occupied by the British, who also settled in Natal and Durban, Boer (Dutch farmers) pioneers traveled north on the "Great Trek" to found the republics of the Transvaal and the Orange Free State, as well as the Cape Colony in Northern Natal. The Union of South Africa was formed in 1910, in 1928 adopting a national flag based on the red, white, and blue tricolor used by the first Dutch settlers.

In 1948, South Africa initiated the policy of apartheid, which was finally abandoned in 1991, and, following the enshrinement of a new, multiracial democracy in the constitution, in 1994 it was decided to adopt a new flag. The flag's design (by the chief herald of South Africa) combines the colors of the Boer republics (red, white, and blue) with those of the African National Congress (black, green, and yellow) and the Zulu Inkhatha Freedom Party (black, green, yellow, red, and white). The pall (the heraldic term for a "Y" shape) that was incorporated into the design symbolizes the convergence of the traditional and the new and signifies the moving together of the South African people toward the future.

SOUTH KOREA

South Korea, whose official name is the Republic of Korea, was formed from the zone south of the 38th Parallel that was occupied by U.S. forces at the end of World War II. The northern zone having been occupied by the U.S.S.R., since 1945 the division between North Korea, or the Democratic People's Republic, and South Korea has been maintained. A U.S. military government administered South Korea from 1945 to 1948, when an independent republic was declared.

The South Korean flag is based on the 19th-century flag of the "united" Korea that was retained, albeit in a slightly altered form, on independence in 1948. The white field represents purity and peace, while the central, blue-and-red disk symbolizes the principles of the "negative" yin (blue) and "positive" yang (red), the concepts of creation and development through duality and balance of Oriental philosophy. The harmonious state of yin and yang is called *Taeguki* in Korean (*Taichi* in Chinese), and *Taeguk-ki* is also the name of the national flag (*ki* means "flag"). The four black *kwae* (trigrams) in each corner, which are drawn from the Chinese book of divination called the *I-Ching* ("Book of Changes"), symbolize the four universal elements. Followed clockwise from the upper hoist, these are *Kun* (heaven), *Yi* (fire), *Kam* (water), and *Kon* (earth).

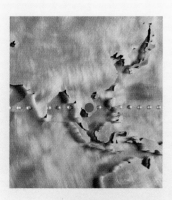

Formal name:
Taehan-min'guk
(Republic of Korea)

Capital city:
Soul (Seoul)

Location:
East Asia

Currency:
I won = 100 jeon

Language:
Korean

Religions:
Buddhist, Protestant, Roman
Catholic, Confucianist

Flag adopted:
September 8, 1948

Flag ratio:
2:3

Formal name:
Reino de España
(Kingdom of Spain)

Capital city:
Madrid

Location:
Western Europe

Currency:
1 Spanish peseta
= 100 céntimos

Languages:
Spanish, Basque, Galician,
Catalan

Religion:
Roman Catholic

Flag adopted:
July 19, 1927

Flag ratio:
2:3

The colors of the Spanish flag are derived from the arms of the provinces of Aragon and Castille. During the 13th century, Spain consisted of a number of small kingdoms that were gradually absorbed by Aragon and Castille. The marriage between Isabella (of Castille) and Ferdinand (of Aragon) in 1469 united Spain, and it soon became a great colonial power.

Spain's first red-and-yellow flag can be traced back to 1785, the result of the wish of the Bourbon king of Spain, Carlos III, to distinguish Spanish warships at sea (the existing war ensign was white and charged with the Bourbon arms, which were easily confused with those of other Bourbon-ruled countries, as well as with the British white ensign). Although not adopted until 1927, these colors have traditionally been associated with Spain.

Republicanism, socialism, and anarchism having vied with each other for power from the late 19th century, in 1931 a republic was established in Spain and a new flag was adopted in the form of a horizontal tricolor of red, yellow, and purple bands of equal width. In 1936, however, a military rebellion led by General Francisco Franco overthrew the republic and restored the yellow-and-red flag. When Franco died, in 1975, King Juan Carlos became head of state, and, for state use, the flag is charged with the national arms, which are set toward the hoist in the yellow band.

SRI LANKA

Formal name:
Shri Lanka Prajatantrika Samajavadi Janarajaya
(Sinhalese appellation)

Ilangi Jananayaka Socialisa Kudiarasu
(Tamil appellation)

(Democratic Socialist Republic of Sri Lanka)

The indigenous people of Sri Lanka (formerly called Ceylon) were the Vedda, who were conquered in about 550 B.C. by Sinhalese from India. During the 3rd century A.D., the island became a world center for Buddhism, the spice trade bringing the Arabs, who called the island *Serendip* ("Serendipity," which means the making of desirable discoveries by accident!) The Europeans, however, called the island Ceylon, and it passed from the Portuguese to the Dutch and finally to Britain (in 1796). Having achieved independence in 1948, in 1972 Ceylon changed its name to Sri Lanka.

The current design of the Sinhalese flag has developed gradually since independence. Originally consisting simply of a golden lion (the Sinhalese word *Sinhala,* meaning "lion," is the basis for the island's name) and a sword on a red field, because it was derived from the emblem of the Sinhalese kingdom of Kandy, it was unpopular with the island's minority groups. It was therefore amended in 1951, when two bands of green (representing Muslims) and orange (representing Tamils) were added. When the country's name changed to Sri Lanka, the flag was altered again, four leaves of the pipul tree (under which Siddhartha sat when he became the Buddha) being added to the four corners of the red panel.

Capital city:
Sri Jayawardenepura (formerly Kotte), (administrative capital), Colombo (commercial capital)

Location:
South Asia/Indian Ocean

Currency:
I Sri Lanka rupee = 100 cents

Languages:
Sinhalese, Tamil, English

Religions:
Buddhist, Hindu, Muslim, Christian

Flag adopted:
December 17, 1978

Flag ratio:
1:2

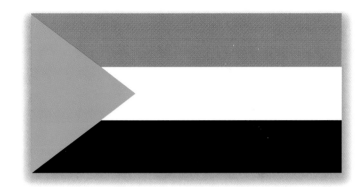

Formal name:
Jumhuryat es-Sudan
(Republic of the Sudan)

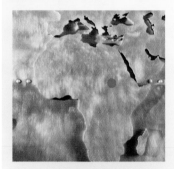

Capital city:
Al Khartum (Khartoum)

Location:
Northeast Africa

Currency:
1 Sudanese dinar = 10
Sudanese pounds

Languages:
Arabic, diverse tribal languages

Religions:
Muslim, Christian, Animist

Flag adopted:
May 20, 1970

Flag ratio:
1:2

In ancient times, Sudan was known as Nubia and formed part of the kingdoms of Upper and Lower Egypt. The Nubians were converted to Coptic Christianity during the 6th century, and, following Arab invasions, to Islam during the 15th century. In 1820, Sudan again came under Egyptian rule, resentment of which led to a revolt in 1881, coordinated by a sheikh who took the title of Mahdi and captured Khartoum in 1895. Having been subdued by an Anglo-Egyptian force, Sudan was administered jointly by Egypt and Britain from 1899 until 1956, when it became an independent republic.

The national flag of the newly independent Sudan was a blue, yellow, and green horizontally striped tricolor. Following a military coup that ousted the government, this flag was abandoned in 1970. Although Sudan remains politically unstable, the country has continued to maintain the national flag that expresses Arab nationalism. The red stripe denotes the blood shed in the struggle for independence, the white band represents peace and optimism, while the black stripe signifies Sudan, also recalling the black flag of the Mahdi uprising of the 19th century. The green at the hoist is a color that is used in many Arab nation's flags: regarded as the favorite color of the Prophet Muhammad, green is the color of Islam.

SURINAM

Formal name:
Republiek Suriname
(Republic of Surinam)

Surinam was settled by English and French traders during the mid-17th century, but became the colony of Dutch Guyana in 1667, when it was ceded to Holland in exchange for New Amsterdam (modern New York) under the terms of the Treaty of Breda. A plantation economy having subsequently been established based on the labor provided by African slaves, when slavery was abolished in 1863, indentured immigrants from China, Java, and India were brought to the colony, creating an ethnic diversity that accounts for Surinam's modern multicultural society.

In 1975, when Surinam gained its independence from the Netherlands, it adopted its current national flag, which replaced the flag that had been flown since 1959, a few years after Surinam had achieved internal self-government. (The earlier flag consisted of a white field on which five stars in the colors white, black, brown, yellow, and red were arranged, the colors signifying Surinam's ethnic diversity.) The flag that was adopted in 1975, which was based on designs sent in by the public, was envisaged as combining the colors of the three main political parties into a design that would symbolize Surinam's unity and progress. As a result, the flag's green, white, and red respectively symbolize fertility, justice, and freedom, while the single, central, golden star is the emblem of national unity.

Capital city:
Paramaribo

Location:
South America

Currency:
1 Surinam guilder = 100 cents

Languages:
Dutch, English, Sranatango
(Taki-Taki)

Religions:
Hindu, Protestant, Muslim,
Roman Catholic

Flag adopted:
November 25, 1975

Flag ratio:
2:3

SWAZILAND

Formal name:
Umbuso we Swatini
(Kingdom of Swaziland)

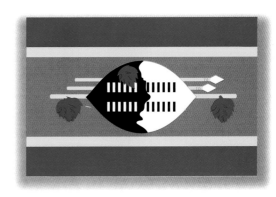

Capital city:
Mbabane

Location:
Southeast Africa

Currency:
1 lilangeni = 100 cents

Languages:
Siswati, English

Religions:
Protestant, Roman Catholic,
Animist

Flag adopted:
October 30, 1967

Flag ratio
2:3

Swaziland's earliest-known inhabitants were the Ndwande people, who lived in the southeast of the region and were defeated during the mid-18th century by the Ngwane, who invaded from the south. The Swazi kingdom was established in the high, central region of the country by the Ngwane people's ruler, Sobhuza I, in 1820. When Europeans settlers arrived during the 1880s, the Swazi granted them concessions, but because these eventually endangered the independence of Swazi territory, in 1894 a joint Anglo-Boer treaty placed Swaziland under the administration of the British governor of Transvaal, thereby guaranteeing the region's autonomy. Although the South African government repeatedly requested control of the region, this was resisted by both the British and the Swazi people. Swaziland became internally self-governing in 1967, and independence followed in 1968, with King Sobhuza II serving as head of state.

The national flag of Swaziland is based on one that was given by the king to the Swazi Pioneer Corps, who served with the British Army during World War II. The central emblem is an Emasotsha warrior's shield, laid horizontally across a staff, from which hang *injobo* tassels made of feathers from the widowbird, a traditional Swazi royal emblem. Above the staff are two *assegai*, Swazi spears.

SWEDEN

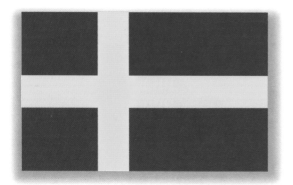

Formal name:
Konungariket Sverige
(Kingdom of Sweden)

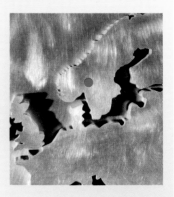

Sweden has been inhabited since around 6000 B.C., its most famous sons perhaps being the Vikings. It became a Christian monarchy during the 10th century, and as result of a series of crusades from the 12th to the 14th centuries, Finland came under Sweden's rule. In 1397, the Danish-dominated Kalmar Union united the crowns of Sweden, Norway, and Denmark. Danish rule was thrown off in 1523, however, during the reign of Gustavus I, the founder of the Vasa royal line which continued to rule until 1818, when Jean-Baptiste Bernadotte, a French marshal, was elected crown prince, succeeding to the throne as Charles XIV. In 1809, Sweden lost Finland to Russia, but annexed Norway in 1814. The union between Sweden and Norway having been dissolved in 1905, the national flag, which had been used in similar form since the 16th century, was formally re-adopted in 1906.

The design of the flag is based on the Scandinavian cross – a cross whose upright arm is not set centrally, but closer to the hoist – which is common to the Norse nations. The distinctive colors of blue and yellow are believed to have been derived from the Swedish national coat of arms, which dates back to the 14th century and features three golden crowns on a blue field.

Capital city:
Stockholm

Location:
Northern Europe

Currency:
1 Swedish krona = 100 öre

Language:
Swedish

Religion:
Lutheran

Flag adopted:
16th century, re-adopted June 22, 1906

Flag ratio:
5:8

SWITZERLAND

Formal name:
Confoederatio Helvetica
(Swiss Confederation)

Capital city:
Bern (Berne)

Location:
Western Europe

Currency:
1 Swiss franc = 100 centimes

Languages:
French, German, Italian,
Romansch

Religions:
Roman Catholic, Protestant

Flag adopted:
December 12, 1889

Flag ratio:
1:1

Despite Switzerland's strategic position between France, Germany, Austria, Liechtenstein, and Italy, throughout its history it has sought to withdraw from, rather than participate in, the power politics of Europe. In 1291, three territories – the "Forest cantons" – Schwyz (which gave its name to the modern country), Uri, and Unterwalden joined together in the Everlasting League to defend their liberty from the Holy Roman Empire. Other cantons subsequently joined the league (there are now 26), and although there was intense rivalry – and often war – between them, the league remained intact. Switzerland's complete independence was recognized by the Treaty of Westphalia in 1648. Having become a democratic federation in 1803, in 1815 the Congress of Vienna guaranteed Swiss neutrality, which is why it has since become the base for many international organizations, such as the Red Cross.

The Swiss flag (which, apart from the Vatican's, is the only square national flag) has been a national emblem since the 14th century and is based on the Schwyz canton's flag. Although the flags of individual cantons continue to be used, the white couped cross on a red field was accepted as the official flag of the Swiss Confederation in 1848. In 1889, the width-to-length ratio of the arms of the cross was altered to its present form.

SYRIA

Formal name:
*Al-Jumhuriyah al-'Arabiyah as-
Suriyah*
(Syrian Arab Republic)

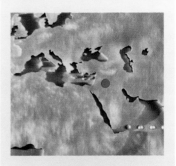

Capital city:
Dimashq (Damascus)

Location:
Western Asia

Currency:
1 Syrian pound = 100 piastres

Languages:
Arabic, Kurdish, Armenian

Religions:
Muslim, Christian

Flag adopted:
March 29, 1980

Flag ratio:
1:2

Ancient Syria was divided up into various small kingdoms that were eventually brought under the control of the mighty Assyrian Empire. Subsequently ruled by the Babylonians, Persians, and Romans, as well as by Byzantium, in A.D. 636 it was conquered by the Saracens. Throughout the Middle Ages, Syria was the scene of many of the battles of the Crusades. Having been part of the Turkish Ottoman Empire from 1516 to 1918, British and French forces occupied the region after World War I. Placed under French mandate in 1920, Syria finally became independent of colonial rule in 1946.

While it was a French colony, Syria flew a green-white-green triband with the French *Tricolore* in the canton. On achieving independence, this flag was changed to a green, white, and black tricolor, with three red stars across the center representing its three provinces. When Syria merged with Egypt to form the United Arab Republic (U.A.R.) in 1958, it adopted the current red, white, and black Pan-Arabic tricolor, but charged it with three stars in anticipation of Iraq joining the U.A.R. Following a military coup in 1961, Syria seceded from the U.A.R. and briefly reverted to the green-white-black tricolor before re-adopting the Pan-Arabic colors in 1963. Since 1980, the Pan-Arabic tricolor, with two green stars, reflecting its original allegiance with Egypt, has been used.

Formal name:
Chung Min Kuo
(Republic of China)

T'ai-wan
(Taiwan)

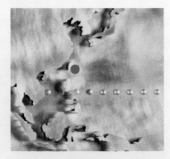

Capital city:
Taipei (temporary) (Taiwan
regards Nanjing (Nanking), on
the Chinese mainland, as its
official capital)

Location:
East Asia

Currency:
1 new Taiwan dollar
= 100 cents

Languages:
Mandarin Chinese, Taiwanese

Religions:
Buddhist, Taoist, Christian,
Confucianist

Flag adopted:
October 8, 1928

Flag ratio:
2:3

Taiwan, or Formosa ("The Beautiful"), was settled by China during the 15th century. It was briefly occupied by the Dutch during the mid-17th century before being annexed by the Chinese Manchu Dynasty in 1683, being ceded to Japan in 1895, following the Sino-Japanese War. Under Chinese control from 1945, in 1949 Taiwan became the refuge for the forces of the Kuomintang (nationalist) government under Chiang Kai-shek, who had fled the People's Republic of China following defeat by the communist troops of Mao Tse-tung.

Taiwan's flag had been the national flag of China while the Kuomintang was in power (from 1928 to 1949), and when the government fled to Taiwan this is the flag it chose. The white sun (symbolizing progress) on the blue canton is the party flag of the Kuomintang, designed by Hou-tung Lu. The red field, added by Sun Yat-sen, represents China itself, the twelve rays that emanate from it denoting a day (the traditional Chinese hour equals two conventional hours). The flag's three colors signify the principles of the people of Taiwan: the blue signifies *Min Chuan* (democracy), the white *Min Sheng* (the people's livelihood), and the red *Min Tsu* (nationalism).

Note *The Taiwanese flag causes offense to the government of the People's Republic of China, and when Taiwan competes in international events, such as the Olympic Games, a sports-association flag, in the national colors and bearing the Olympic emblem, is used.*

TAJIKISTAN

Formal name:
Jumhurii Todhzikiston
(Republic of Tajikistan)

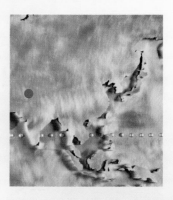

The Tajiks, an Iranian people, were subjects of the Persian Empire until the 8th century, when the Arabs extended their influence over the area. During the 13th century, Mongol invaders swept through Asia, and the region became part of the empire of Tamerlane (Timur) and his descendants. Conquered by czarist Russia in 1860, the Soviet Red Army occupied the Tajik homeland in 1920. Although Tajik revolts continued to simmer from 1922, in 1929 the Tajik (Persian-speaking) areas of Bukhara and Turkestan were joined within a union republic of the U.S.S.R.

After gaining its independence in 1991, Tajikistan was the last of the former Soviet socialist republics to adopt a new flag. The colors chosen are the same as those of the Tajik Soviet Republic flag that was used from 1953 to 1992. The red stripe represents socialism, while the white stripe symbolizes cotton, Tajikistan's major industrial product, and the green stripe the region's other agricultural products. (These colors may have been influenced by the Iranian flag, the Tajiks being the only former members of a Central Asian Soviet republic to speak a Persian-related language.) Although the stylized crown in the center of the white stripe is said to represent Tajikistan's sovereignty, the significance of the seven stars is unknown.

Capital city:
Dushanbe

Location:
Central Asia

Currency:
1 rouble = 100 kopecks

Languages:
Tajik, Uzbek, Russian

Religion:
Sunni Muslim

Flag adopted:
November 24, 1992

Flag ratio:
1:2

TANZANIA

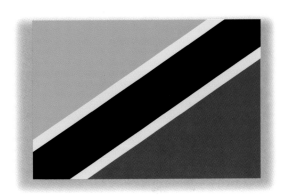

Formal name:
*Jumhuri ya Mwungano was
Tanzania*
United Republic of Tanzania

Capital city:
Dodoma

Location:
East Africa

Currency:
I Tanzanian shilling = I00 cents

Languages;
Swahili, English
(official languages), diverse
Bantu languages

Religions:
Roman Catholic, Muslim,
Animist

Flag adopted:
June 30, 1964

Flag ratio:
2:3

Tanzania's coast had been explored during the 8th century by Arabs, but it was the arrival of Vasco da Gama on its shores in 1498 that heralded its rulership by the Portuguese until their expulsion by Omani Arabs in 1698. Having been a colony of German East Africa from 1884, mainland Tanzania became the British trust territory of Tanganyika in 1919 and an independent state in 1961. Nearby Zanzibar, famed for its spices and the largest coral island off the coast of Africa, having united with the nearby island of Pemba, similarly became an Omani possession from the late 18th century until 1856, when a British protectorate was established. In 1963, the sultan of Zanzibar was overthrown and the islands became independent. In 1964, the United Republic of Tanzania was formed when Tanganyika and Zanzibar were united, the name of the new republic reflecting the union.

Tanzania's new flag likewise merged parts of the flags of both Tanganyika and Zanzibar. Green and black – the colors of the Tanganyikan African National Union, the dominant political party – and the green, black, and blue colors of the Afro-Shirazi Party, which overthrew the sultan of Zanzibar, were used, the stripes being arranged diagonally to give each equal status. Yellow fimbriations were added to the black stripe to symbolize the nation's mineral wealth, especially its diamonds, coal, and iron.

THAILAND

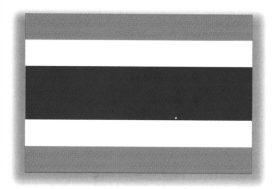

Formal name:
Prathet Thai
(Kingdom of Thailand)

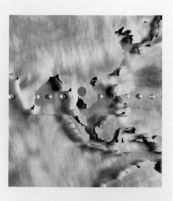

Although known locally as Muang Thai, "Land of the Free," Thailand was called Siam until 1939. The Thai people originated in Yunnan (China), moving south after their capital, Nanchao, was destroyed by the Mongols in 1253. Having seized the Khmer city of Sukhothai, in 1350 the Thai made it the center of their new kingdom, the astute diplomacy of their rulers subsequently enabling Thailand to resist European attempts at colonization. The present royal dynasty, the Chakkri, was founded in 1782 by Rana I, who moved his capital to Bangkok.

A plain, red flag charged with a white elephant was flown during the 19th century, reflecting the country's epithet, "Land of the White Elephant." In 1916, during World War I, horizontal white stripes were added above and below the elephant. The current flag, or *Thong Chat Thai,* was devised in 1917 by King Vajiravudh-Rama VI, who removed the elephant emblem and added a blue stripe at the center to create the *Trairong* (tricolor). It is said that he did this to express Siam's solidarity with the Allies, although the prevailing view is that the blue stripe symbolizes the monarchy. The two outer, red stripes are said to represent the land, while the white stripes symbolize the Theravada Buddhist faith.

Capital city:
Krung Thep (Bangkok)

Location:
Southeast Asia

Currency:
1 Thai baht = 100 satang

Languages:
Thai, Chinese, Malay

Religions:
Buddhist, Muslim

Flag adopted:
September 28, 1917

Flag ratio:
2:3

Formal name:
Po
(Autonomous Region of Tibet)

DISPUTED FLAG

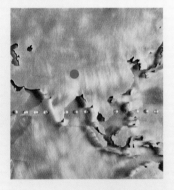

Capital city:
Lhasa

Location:
Asia

Currency:
1 yuan = 10 jiao = 100 fen

Languages:
Tibetan, Chinese

Religion:
Buddhist

An independent state from the 5th century, Tibet was for centuries a theocracy (state governed by religious leaders) under the leadership of Buddhist lamas, or monks. Tibet came under Chinese rule in 1700, regaining its independence only in 1912, after a revolt. China regained control of Tibet in 1951, however, and in 1959 the Dalai Lama (the spiritual leader of Tibetan Buddhism and the head of Tibet's government), along with some 9,000 Tibetans, fled to India during a revolt against Chinese rule. China dissolved Tibet's local government and replaced it with a ruler that was sympathetic to it, also making Tibet an autonomous region of China.

The flag illustrated is used by the Tibetan government-in-exile, as well as Tibetan organizations throughout the world. Its use in Tibet is forbidden, however, while flying it elsewhere is regarded as offensive by the Chinese authorities.

TOGO

Formal name:
République du Togo
(Republic of Togo)

Togoland was a German protectorate until 1914, when it was divided between France and Britain. Joint rule continued under a United Nations' mandate until 1956, when British Togoland voted for integration with Ghana and French Togoland opted to become an autonomous republic within the French union, achieving full independence in 1960 as the Republic of Togo.

A competition to design a new flag for the new Togo was announced by the Togolese government in 1958, which was won by Ahyi Paul. Like many of the African nations that won their independence at that time, Togo's flag uses the colors of Pan-Africanism. The five green and yellow stripes, which represent the five regions of the country (Régions Maritime, Plateaux, Centrale, de la Kara, and des Savanes), are said to equate to the five fingers of a hand, thus symbolizing action. The yellow stripes signify both national unity and the country's mineral wealth, the green represents agriculture, while the red of the canton denotes the blood shed in the struggle for independence. The five-pointed star that emerges from the red of the canton symbolizes the liberty gained on the attainment of independence, its white color signifying peace and wisdom.

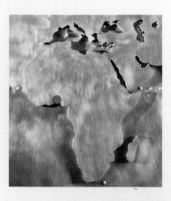

Capital city:
Lomé

Location:
West Africa

Currency:
1 C.F.A. franc = 100 centimes

Languages:
French, Ewe, Kabye

Religions:
Christian, Muslim, Animist

Flag adopted:
April 27, 1960

Flag ratio:
2:3

Formal name:
Pule'anga Tonga
(Kingdom of Tonga)

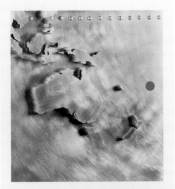

Capital city:
Nuku'alofa

Location:
Pacific Ocean

Currency:
1 pa'anga = 100 seniti

Languages:
English, Tongan

Religions:
Protestant, Roman Catholic

Flag adopted:
November 4, 1875

Flag ratio
1:2

Tonga consists of more than 150 islands spread over more than 140,000 square miles (approximately 350,000 square kilometers), although only 40 of the islands are inhabited. Tonga was first settled by Polynesians, possibly from Fiji, around 3,500 years ago. When the British explorer Captain James Cook visited Tonga in 1773, he dubbed it the "Friendly Islands" on account of the warm welcome that he received. Wesleyan Methodist ministers having arrived from England during the early 19th century, the paramount chief, Taufa'ahau Tupou (who became known as King George Tupou I, the founder of the contemporary Tongan royal dynasty), was converted to Christianity in 1831. Made a British protectorate in 1900 – but never a colony – Tonga became independent in 1970.

In 1862, at the behest of King George Tupou I, a flag expressing Tonga's conversion to Christianity was flown, but because it turned out to be identical to the flag of the International Red Cross, in order to avoid confusion, it was altered so that the former flag appeared as the canton of a Red Ensign. The red cross represents Tonga's Christian faith, and the red field Christ's blood. The design of the new flag was credited to Prince Uelingatoni Ngu Tupoumalohi and a Methodist minister, Reverend Shirley Baker, and the 1875 Tonga constitution states that it shall never be altered.

TRINIDAD AND TOBAGO

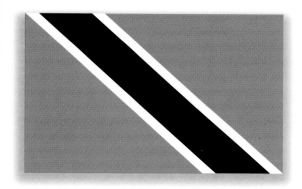

Formal name:
Republic of Trinidad and Tobago

Trinidad was inhabited by the Igneri people, and the volcanic island of Tobago by the Caribs, when the adjacent islands, situated off the coast of Venezuela, were discovered by Christopher Columbus in 1498. Although the northern island of Tobago was claimed by the Spanish, it subsequently became a possession of the British, Dutch, and French in turn, until 1814, when it was returned to Britain. Trinidad, to the south, was settled by the Dutch and French, but was ceded to Britain in 1802. In 1899, the two islands merged to form a single colony, which achieved full independence in 1962.

The flag of Trinidad and Tobago, which dates from the year of independence, was chosen from designs submitted by the public. The red, white, and black colors that feature in the flag are highly symbolic. Red denotes the vitality of the land and people, as well as the warmth and energy of the sun; white signifies the sea that unites the two islands, and also conveys the purity of the nation's hopes; and the black diagonal symbolizes the strength, unity, and purpose of the people. The colors also represent the three elements of fire (red), earth (black), and water (white) that together constitute the islands.

Capital city:
Port of Spain

Location:
Caribbean

Currency:
1 Trinidad and Tobago dollar =
100 cents

Languages:
English, Spanish, Hindi, Creole

Religions:
Roman Catholic, Protestant,
Hindu, Muslim

Flag adopted:
August 31, 1962

Flag ratio:
3:5

Formal name:

Al Jumhriyah al-Tunisiyah
(Republic of Tunisia)

Capital city:
Tunis

Location:
North Africa

Currency:
1 Tunisian dinar = 1000
millimes

Languages:
Arabic, French

Religion:
Muslim, Christian

Flag adopted:
1835

Flag ratio:
2:3

The Phoenicians founded Carthage (near Tunis) during the 8th century B.C., the Carthaginian Empire subsequently falling to Rome during the Punic Wars. The area passed to the Byzantine Empire in A.D. 533, but Arab invasions won Tunisia for the Islamic world in 647. Tunisia was part of the Ottoman Empire from 1574 until 1881, when it became a French protectorate, the *bey* (monarch) remaining as nominal ruler. Nationalist sentiment grew during the 20th century, however, until independence was finally gained in 1956. The monarchy was abolished in the following year and Tunisia was proclaimed a republic.

The Tunisian flag is based on the flag of its former rulers, the Ottoman Turks. Adopted by the *bey* in 1835, and used primarily for military purposes, during the period of French colonial rule it served as a naval flag with the French *Tricolore* in the canton. When Tunisia became independent, the original flag was restored. The white disk in the center of the red field represents the sun and contains two Islamic symbols: a red, five-pointed star and a red *Osmanli* (Turkish crescent). When seen from the point of view of an Arabic reader of the flag (i.e., from right to left), the shape of the moon is said to bring good fortune.

TURKEY

Formal name:
Türkiye Cumhuriyeti
(Republic of Turkey)

The Republic of Turkey was established in 1923 from the remnants of the Ottoman Empire, which, following its foundation by Sultan Osman I in 1299, conquered Asia Minor, the Balkans, North Africa, Egypt, Syria, Arabia, Mesopotamia and, by 1550, most of Hungary. By 1918, however, its rule was over.

The red of the current Turkish flag's field was the predominant color of Ottoman Turkish flags for more than seven-hundred years, and there are many legends explaining the origin of the star-and-crescent emblem that also appears on the flag. One explanation is that the moon was the emblem of the Roman goddess Diana, the patron of Byzantium (later Constantinople and today Istanbul, the capital of the Byzantine Empire before its defeat by the Ottoman Empire) and that when, in A.D. 330, the Roman Emperor Constantine rededicated the city to the Virgin Mary, he added the star in her honor. Whatever their origin, the crescent moon and star have long been the symbols of Islam, and continued to be used in Turkey after a secular republic had been declared. The basic form of the Turkish flag, known to its people as *ay yildiz* ("Moon Star"), was established by Sultan Selim III in 1793, when existing green naval flags were changed to red and white and a crescent and eight-pointed star were added. The five-pointed star dates from 1844, and this version was retained by President Mustafa Kemel (Atatürk) in 1923, being ratified in 1936.

Capital city:
Ankara

Location:
Eastern Europe/Western Asia

Currency:
I Turkish lira = 100 kurus

Languages:
Turkish

Religion:
Sunni Muslim

Flag adopted:
in use since 1844, officially
adopted June 5, 1936

Flag ratio:
2:3

TURKMENISTAN

Formal name:
Turkmenostan Respublikasy
(Republic of Turkmenistan)

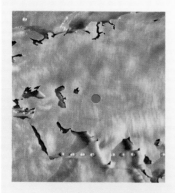

Capital city:
Ashkhabad (Ashgabat)

Location:
Central Asia

Currency:
1 manat

Languages:
Turkmen, Russian, Uzbek

Religion:
Sunni Muslim

Flag adopted:
January 30, 1997

Flag ratio:
1:2

The nomadic Turkmen tribes are the Tekkes of Merv and Attok, Esaris, Yomuds, and the Gokluns, who all speak varieties of a Turkic language and are the descendants of the Mongols who swept across Asia during the 13th century. From the 15th to the 17th centuries, the southern part of Turkmenistan was ruled by the Persians, while the north was controlled by the Uzbek khans (rulers) of Khiva and Bukhara. Despite formidable opposition from the Turkmen tribes, czarist Russian troops systematically conquered the region between 1877 and 1900. Although Turkmenistan resisted communist rule following the Russian Revolution of 1917, by 1925 the Turkmen Soviet Socialist Republic had become a constituent of the U.S.S.R. Turkmenistan finally proclaimed its independence after the breakup of the U.S.S.R. in October 1991, adopting a new national flag in 1992.

In the hoist of a plain, green flag bearing a white crescent and stars (symbolizing Islam) were placed five *guls* (traditional carpet designs) on a red stripe. Turkmenistan is famous for its carpets, and each *gul* represents one of the Turkmen tribes. Following the resolution of the United Nations (U.N.) in 1995 that Turkmenistan would remain permanently neutral, on January 29, 1997 an olive branch, identical to that on the UN flag, was added to the bottom *gul* to celebrate Turkmenistan's new status.

TUVALU

The group of nine islands that we now know as Tuvalu was part of Britain's colony of the Gilbert and Ellice Islands from 1915 until 1975, when the Ellice Islands separated from the Gilbert Islands (now Kiribati) and adopted the new name of Tuvalu, Tuvalu becoming independent in 1978.

Since independence, Tuvalu has flown two different flags. The first flag was a pale version of the Blue Ensign, reflecting Tuvalu's historic links with the United Kingdom. The pale blue of the field, which also symbolized the islands' tropical ocean surroundings, was charged with nine golden stars, representing the nine islands of Tuvalu. (The name "Tuvalu," which was adopted when only eight of the nine islands were inhabited, means "Eight Islands," or "Eight Standing Together.") The nine stars were arranged in the fly to show the islands' geographical relationship. In 1995, anti-Commonwealth feeling became intense, however, and the Tuvalu government decided to adopt a new flag consisting of three bands of red, blue, and red separated by white fimbriations. In place of the British Union Jack, a white triangle with the islands' arms was added to the blue band in the hoist, the number of stars also being reduced to eight, consistent with the islands' name. In 1997, a new administration decided to re-adopt the 1978 design for Tuvalu's national flag.

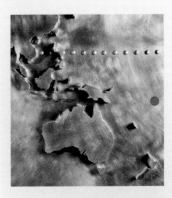

Formal name:
Tuvalu

Capital city:
Funafuti

Location:
Pacific Ocean

Currency:
1 Australian dollar = 100 cents

Languages:
Tuvaluan, English

Religions:
Protestant, Ba'hai, Muslim

Flag adopted:
October 1, 1978

Flag ratio:
1:2

Formal name:
Republic of Uganda

Capital city:
Kampala

Location:
East Africa

Currency:
1 Uganda shilling = 100 cents

Languages:
English, Luganda

Religions:
Roman Catholic, Protestant, Animist, Muslim

Flag adopted:
October 9, 1962

Flag ratio:
2:3

Established in 1894, the British protectorate of Uganda was centered around the powerful African kingdom of Buganda. It became independent in 1962 and was proclaimed a federal republic in 1963, although the ruling Bugandan *kabaka* (king), Edward Mutesa II, became the republic's first president, ruling through a cabinet. The king was deposed (as president; he remained king) in a coup in 1966, after which the country was ruled by two dictatorial regimes, first that of Milton Obote (from 1966 to 1971, who ended the country's federal status) and then that of Idi Amin (from 1971 to 1978), before democratic and economic reforms were introduced during the mid-1980s.

The design of the newly independent Uganda's national flag was suggested by the minister of justice, Mr. Grace Ibingira. Although the black, yellow, and red stripes were intended to symbolize the people of Africa (black), the sunshine of the land (yellow), and the brotherhood of the people (red), these colors were also those of the Uganda People's Congress (U.P.C.), the dominant political party in Uganda at the time of independence. The Ugandan flag is an adaptation of the U.P.C. tricolor, with the addition of a central, white disk bearing a great crested crane, an emblem that was used as Uganda's colonial badge during the period of British rule.

UKRAINE

Formal name:
Ukrayina (Ukraine)

The second-largest country in Europe (after Russia), Ukraine formed the heartland of the medieval state of Kievan Rus that emerged during the 9th century. Having united with Russians (Muscovites) and Belorussians, it subsequently became the leading power in Eastern Europe before being conquered by the Mongols during the 13th century. It came under Polish rule from the 14th century until 1648, when a Cossack-led revolt established a military state. During the late 18th century, czarist Russia secured control of Ukraine, but, following the Russian Revolution of 1917, an independent Ukrainian People's Republic was declared in 1918.

The flag that the Ukrainian People's Republic adopted consisted of two equal-sized, horizontal bands, blue over yellow, the traditional colors of the Kievan Rus and, unusually for a Slavic state, not the Pan-Slavic colors. The blue represents the sky, while the yellow signifies the fields of golden grain that dominate Ukraine's landscape. This flag was retained until the Soviet Red Army invaded Ukraine in 1921, and when Ukraine became a union republic of the U.S.S.R. in 1922, a "Red Flag" was flown. Following the dissolution of the U.S.S.R. in 1991, Ukraine once again declared its independence and re-adopted the blue-and-yellow flag that was first used in 1918.

Capital city:
Kyiv (Kiev)

Location:
Eastern Europe

Currency:
1 hryvnya = 100 kopiyky

Languages:
Ukrainian, Russian, Polish, Tatar

Religions:
Ukrainian Orthodox, Uniate
(Greek Catholic)

Flag adopted:
September 4, 1991

Flag ratio:
2:3

Formal name:
Al-Imrata al-Arabiyyah al-Muttahida
(United Arab Emirates)

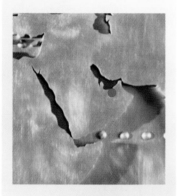

Capital city:
Abu Zaly (Abu Dhabi)

Location:
Southwest Asia

Currency:
1 U.A.E. dirham = 100 fils

Language:
Arabic

Religion:
Muslim

Flag adopted:
December 2, 1971

Flag ratio:
1:2

Previously called the Trucial States, the United Arab Emirates (U.A.E.) is a federation of independent states situated on the Arabian Peninsula. Seven emirates make up the U.A.E.: Abu Dhabi (the capital of the U.A.E. is located in the emirate of the same name), 'Ajman, Dubai, Al-Fujayrah, Ra's al-Khaymah, Sharjah, and Umm al-Qaywayn. Because the states occupied a strategic position on the trade route to India, during the 19th century Britain signed a series of *truces* (treaties) with the ruling emirs to bring the Trucial States under British protection.

Although each emirate maintained its individual red flag of the Kharijite Muslims (white being added at British request in 1820 to distinguish them from pirates' flags), in 1968, in an attempt to form a Federation of Arab Emirates (which would have included Bahrain and Kuwait), a flag consisting of horizontal stripes in the order red-white-red, bearing a green, seven-pointed star in the center, was adopted. (A proposed nine-pointed star was dropped when Kuwait and Bahrain did not join the federation.) When the Trucial States became independent as the United Arab Emirates in 1971, a federal flag in the Pan-Arabic colors of red, green, white, and black was adopted to express the U.A.E.'s unity and nationalism. Locally, however, each emirate continues to use its own flag and arms, except for the emirate of Sharjah, which flies the U.A.E. flag.

UNITED KINGDOM

Although popularly called the "Union Jack," the correct name of the British flag is the Union Flag. Despite being flown by such a small country (roughly the size of Colorado), the British flag is one of the world's most familiar, largely due to the seminal role that Britain has played in world history, and perhaps also on account of its unusual design. The British flag consists of a blue field, a counterchanged red-and-white saltire cross (note how the red arms of the diagonal cross change position), on which is superimposed a vertical, red cross.

The first version of the Union Flag appeared in 1603, when the Scottish and English crowns were united on the accession to the English throne of King James VI of Scotland as King James I of England. Although both countries retained their own flags (and continue to do so to this day), James decided that a new flag was needed to confirm the union, ordering the red St. George's Cross of England (which included Wales) to be combined with the white (on a blue field) St. Andrew's cross of Scotland. When Ireland (whose flag was the red saltire cross of St. Patrick on a white field) joined the newly created United Kingdom of Great Britain and Ireland in 1801, it was decided to counterchange the colors of the saltire crosses so that it did not appear that the St. Andrew's cross was a mere fimbriation for the St. Patrick's cross, thus making them equal. Perhaps surprisingly, the Union Flag has never officially been adopted by law.

Formal name:
United Kingdom of Great Britain and Northern Ireland

Capital city:
London

Location
Western Europe

Currency:
1 pound sterling = 100 pence

Languages:
English, Welsh, Scots Gaelic, Irish Gaelic
(all official languages), plus diverse other languages

Religions:
Protestant, Roman Catholic, Muslim, Hindu, Jewish, Buddhist, plus diverse other religions

Flag adopted:
January 1, 1801

Flag ratio:
1:2

UNITED STATES OF AMERICA

Formal name:
United States of America

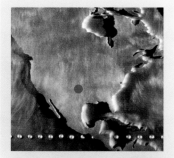

Capital city:
Washington, D.C.

Location:
North America

Currency:
1 U.S. dollar = 100 cents

Languages:
English, Spanish, plus diverse
other languages

Religion:
Protestant, Roman Catholic,
Jewish, Muslim, plus diverse
other religions

Flag adopted:
July 4, 1960

Flag ratio:
10:19

The United States of America, a federal republic of 50 states, was formed when 13 British colonies in North America rose against the British government in 1775. Led by General George Washington, they defeated the troops of King George III during the American Revolution, declaring their independence on July 4, 1776.

The U.S. flag was based on the "Grand Union Flag," which had 13 stripes of red and white (representing the colonies), along with the British flag of the time in the canton. In 1777, following the achievement of independence, the Union Jack was removed and replaced with a blue canton containing 13 stars representing the 13 states. Two new states having joined the union in 1795, the flag (which was now known as the "Star-spangled Banner") was altered to comprise 15 stars and 15 stripes. Although five more states joined the union after this date, the flag remained unchanged until 1817, when Congress decreed that the flag should revert to the original 13 stripes, but that new stars should be added as the union grew. In 1818, the flag therefore had 13 stripes and 20 stars. The most recent stars were added for Alaska (1959) and Hawaii (1960), bringing the total number of states, and stars on the "Stars and Stripes," to 50. Each state (and U.S. overseas territory) also flies its own flag.

URUGUAY

Formal name:
República Oriental del Uruguay
(Eastern Republic of Uruguay)

Uruguay was settled by both the Spanish (in 1624) and the Portuguese (in 1680), but became part of Spain's colonial empire during the 18th century. Between 1808 (when it declared its independence from Spain) and 1830 (when complete independence was achieved), Uruguay struggled to maintain its independent status. The struggle for independence was led by the national hero José Artigas (who flew a blue-and-white-striped flag with a red diagonal band known as the *Banda Oriental*, or the "East Bank," of Uruguay). Although Spanish rule was overthrown in 1814, Artigas was driven out of Uruguay in 1820 by Brazilian forces, who annexed the country. The region continued to be disputed by Brazil and Argentina, with both countries lending support to the opposing political factions that sought to control the region.

Until 1830, when, following international mediation, Uruguay was established as an independent nation, variations of Artigas's flag were flown. On achieving independence, however, Uruguay formally adopted a new national flag made up of nine stripes in blue and white (the country's national colors), representing the country's nine original provinces. The "Sun of May" emblem, which has been Uruguay's national emblem since 1815, appears on the white canton.

Capital city:
Montevideo

Location:
South America

Currency:
1 Uruguayan peso = 100
céntesimos

Language:
Spanish

Religion:
Roman Catholic

Flag adopted:
July 11, 1830

Flag ratio:
2:3

UZBEKISTAN

Formal name:
Uzbekiston Respublikasi
(Republic of Uzbekistan)

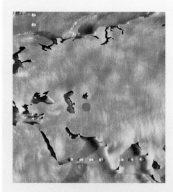

Capital city:
Tashkent

Location:
Central Asia

Currency:
I som = 100 tiyin

Languages:
Uzbek, Russian

Religion:
Sunni Muslim

Flag adopted:
November 18, 1991

Flag ratio:
1:2

Ruled by the Arabs from the 8th century, during the 13th century the Mongols invaded the area that we now know as Uzbekistan, Tamerlane (Timur) establishing the Mongolian Empire's capital at Samarkand. The Uzbek khanates (states) of Bukhara and Khiva were founded during the 15th and 16th centuries, Persia ruling part of the region during the 18th century before it was conquered in part by czarist Russia in 1876. Following the Russian Revolution of 1917, the Tashkent Soviet gradually extended its power, eventually deposing the ruling emirs. Having become a republic of the U.S.S.R. in 1925, following the breakup of the Soviet Union in 1991, Uzbekistan became the first Central Asian Republic to declare its sovereignty and adopt postcommunist national symbols.

The colors of the Uzbek blue-white-green-striped national flag are symbolic. The blue signifies the sky and water, and was also the color of Tamerlane's flag; the white represents peace and purity; the red fimbriations denote the people's life force; and the green is the traditional color of Islam, the religion of the Uzbek people. A white crescent and 12 white stars are arranged in the upper hoist corner. Although Uzbekistan is a Muslim country, and the crescent moon is an Islamic symbol, in the context of the flag the symbol is said to denote the rebirth of the nation, while the stars represent the signs of the zodiac.

VANUATU

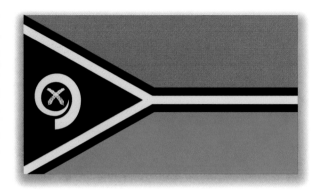

Consisting of more than eighty islands forming a "Y" shape in the southwestern Pacific Ocean, from 1906 until 1980, when it gained its independence, Vanuatu (then named the New Hebrides, as it was first dubbed by the British explorer Captain James Cook, who arrived there in 1774) was jointly administered by Britain and France.

Before it became independent, Vanuatu flew the French *Tricolore* alongside the British "Union Jack." In 1980, the flag that would represent the new nation was chosen by a committee from designs submitted by a local artist. Although its yellow, green, red, and black colors were derived from the flag of the English-speaking Vanua'aka Party, which led Vanuatu to independence, they also have their own significance. The yellow symbolizes sunshine and Christianity, also forming the islands' "Y" shape; the green denotes the islands' rich vegetation; the red signifies both blood (particularly that of the sacrificial boar) and the power of tradition; while the black represents the Melanesian people. The black triangle contains a boar's curled tusk, a symbol of prosperity that is worn as a pendant on the islands (pigs traditionally constitute wealth among the islanders, and spiral tusks apparently only grow on hand-fed pigs). Contained within the tusk are two crossed fronds of a local *namele* fern that symbolize peace, their 39 divisions furthermore representing the 39 members of Vanuatu's legislative assembly.

Formal name:
Ripablik blong Vanuatu
(Republic of Vanuatu)

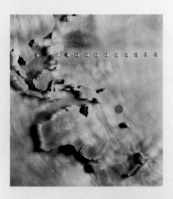

Capital city:
Port-Vila (Vila)

Location:
Pacific Ocean

Currency:
1 vatu = 100 centimes

Languages:
Bislama, French, and over a hundred Melanesian languages

Religions:
Protestant, Roman Catholic

Flag adopted:
February 18, 1980

Flag ratio
3:5

VATICAN CITY

Formal name:
Stato della Città del Vaticano
(Vatican City State)

Capital city:
The Vatican

Location:
sovereign area within the City
of Rome, Italy

Currency:
own currency equal to the
Italian lira

Language:
Latin (official language), Italian

Religion:
Roman Catholic

Flag adopted:
introduced in 1825, official
since June 8, 1929

Flag ratio:
1:1

The Vatican City State, which occupies 110 acres (44 hectares) of sovereign land within the City of Rome, Italy, is the smallest independent country in the world. The kingdom of Italy having been proclaimed in 1861, in 1870 France withdrew the troops from Rome that it had sent to protect the pope during Italy's unification struggle, whereupon Italian forces entered the city, which subsequently became the capital of Italy. Pope Pius IX (who reigned between 1846 and 1878) protested his loss of temporal power by retreating into the Vatican, a papal residence since 1377. In 1929, the Lateran Treaty finally reconciled the Italian government with the Roman Catholic Church, the Vatican City being recognized as an independent state.

Although the papal colors were historically red and gold, in 1808 Pope Pius VII (who reigned from 1800 to 1823) chose the new colors of yellow (gold) and silver (white), which are said to be those of St. Peter's keys to the gates of heaven. A square, bicolored, yellow-white flag, with St. Peter's keys in the white fly stripe supporting the papal crown (the three tiers of which denote the three types of temporal power vested in the pope: legislative, executive, and judicial) was adopted in 1825 and used until 1870. The flag was reintroduced in 1929, when Italy granted the Vatican City its independent status.

VENEZUELA

Formal name:
República Bolivariana de Venezuela
(Bolivarian Republic of Venezuela)

Christopher Columbus having visited Venezuela in 1498, the first Spanish settlement was established there in 1520, and it remained a Spanish colony for more than three-hundred years. Venezuela was finally liberated by the South American nationalist, Simón Bolívar, in 1819, joining Colombia, Ecuador, and Panama in the new state of Greater Colombia.

Like those of Colombia and Ecuador, Venezuela's flag is based on the tricolor of Francisco de Miranda, the initiator of the 1806 revolt against Spain in the province of New Granada. This flag was a plain tricolor of yellow, blue, and red horizontal bands that symbolized the ocean (the middle, blue band) that separated the Americas (red) from the Spanish rulers (yellow). As a member of Greater Colombia, Venezuela continued to fly a yellow, blue, and red tricolor, although with a double-width yellow stripe. In 1830, when Venezuela seceded from Greater Colombia and became a republic, the stripes of the flag reverted to equal widths, the colors now being said to symbolize the richness of the region (yellow), the sea (blue), and the blood of the patriots shed during the struggle for independence (red). The flag remained a plain tricolor until 1836, when seven stars representing Barinas, Barcelona, Caracas, Cumana, Margarita, Merida, and Trujillo (the seven provinces that had joined the revolt against Spain) were added.

Capital city:
Caracas

Location:
South America

Currency:
1 bolivar = 100 céntimos

Language:
Spanish

Religion:
Roman Catholic

Flag adopted:
April 20, 1836

Flag ratio:
2:3

Formal name:
Công Hòa Xã Hôi Chu Nghia Viêt Nam
(Socialist Republic of Vietnam)

Capital city:
Hanoi

Location:
Southeast Asia

Currency:
1 dông = 10 hao = 100 xu

Languages:
Vietnamese, Chinese

Religions:
Buddhist, Roman Catholic

Flag adopted:
November 30, 1955

Flag ratio:
2:3

Vietnam, which was founded in 208 B.C. in the Red River Delta, remained under direct Chinese rule until A.D. 939, when Tongkin and Annam broke free to establish an independent Vietnamese state. France established a protectorate in the region during the 1860s, by 1887 having established the Union of Indochina (made up of Vietnam, Laos, and Cambodia). Resistance to French rule having begun during the 1930s, however, nationalist forces under Ho Chi Minh secured Vietnam's independence in 1954, following an eight-year war. The country was now partitioned into two zones: the communist North Vietnam and the pro-Western South Vietnam. For the next twenty years, South Vietnam, supported by the United States, waged war against North Vietnam, which was seeking to unify the country. The U.S. having withdrawn its troops in 1973, South Vietnam fell to the communist offensive in 1975, the unified Socialist Republic of Vietnam being declared in 1976.

Since 1976, North Vietnam's red flag, which is charged with a yellow star, has flown over the entire country. The red of the field stands for the blood shed by the Vietnamese people during the revolution, while the five points of the star represent the workers, peasants, thinkers, youths, and soldiers who built up socialism in Vietnam.

WESTERN SAHARA

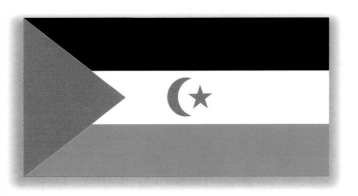

Formal name:
*Al Jumhuriyah al'Arabiyah al
Dimuqratiyah al Sahrawi*
(Democratic Arab Republic of
Sahara)

DISPUTED FLAG

Capital city:
Laayoune

Location:
Northwest Africa

Languages:
Arabic, Spanish

Formerly called Spanish Sahara, the region now known as Western Sahara was an overseas province of Spain from 1958 to 1976, when it was partitioned between Mauritania and Morocco (which took the greater part of the territory). In protest, the Popular Front for the Liberation of Saguia el Hamra and Rio de Oro (the country's two provinces), or P.O.L.I.S.A.R.I.O., declared an independent republic on February 27, 1976. Mauritania withdrew from the region in 1979, whereupon Morocco absorbed the sector that it had vacated. P.O.L.I.S.A.R.I.O. continued to wage a guerrilla campaign against Morocco, which built a sand-and-rock wall 9 feet (3 meters) high and 2,000 miles (3,200 kilometers) long around Western Sahara. Informal talks brokered by the United Nations between the Sahrawis (the indigenous population of Western Sahara) and Morocco began in 1988. Although a ceasefire and referendum on the future of Western Sahara was agreed in 1991, no date has yet been set for either.

Because of the disputed status of the territory, the flag illustrated here is unofficial. It is, however, used to represent Western Sahara within the Organization of African Unity (O.A.U.) to which it was admitted as a member in 1982.

Formal name:
Al-Jumhuriyah al-Yamaniyah
(Republic of Yemen)

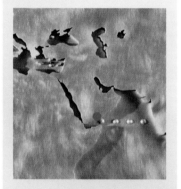

Capital city:
San'a

Location:
Southwest Asia

Currency:
1 Yemeni dinar = 26 riyals,
1 rial = 100 fils

Language:
Arabic

Religion:
Muslim

Flag adopted:
May 22, 1990

Flag ratio:
2:3

The Ottoman Turks once occupied the area that we now know as Yemen, not being expelled until 1911, when Imam Yahya secured its independence. The first flag of the independent Yemen was red, with a white sword arranged horizontally and five white stars, representing the five duties of a devout Muslim.

Britain, which had established Aden as a staging post to India in 1839, now gradually established control over Yemen's southern region, the Aden Protectorate being formally instituted in 1937. In 1962, armed rebellion against British rule led to a republican movement in the north forming the Yemen Arab Republic (Y.A.R.), commonly called North Yemen, while independence for the south was won in 1967 as the People's Democratic Republic of Yemen (P.D.R.Y.), generally called South Yemen. From 1963 through 1986, the two rival Yemens were often engaged in civil war until, in 1990, the Republic of Yemen was created as a result of their peaceful unification.

Prior to unification, both countries used flags modeled on the Egyptian Pan-Arabic flag, in that both were red, black, and white tricolors. The flag of the secular and socialist South Yemen carried a blue triangle (representing the Yemeni people) and red star of socialism, however, while the flag of Islamic North Yemen bore a green, five-pointed star in the central white stripe, symbolizing Arab unity. On unification, both emblems were dropped from the new national flag.

YUGOSLAVIA

Formal name:
Savezna Republika Jugoslavija
(Federal Republic of Yugoslavia)

Having once been ruled by the Ottoman and Austro-Hungarian empires, a kingdom of Serbs, Croats, and Slovenes was formed in December 1918, with Montenegro joining soon afterward. In 1929, under the Serbian king, Alexander I, the country was renamed Yugoslavia, meaning "Land of the Southern Slavs." After World War II, Josip Broz (Marshal Tito), the leader of the country's resistance movement, proclaimed the formation of the Yugoslav Federal Republic, which consisted of Bosnia and Herzegovina, Croatia, Macedonia, Montenegro, Serbia, and Slovenia. Ethnic tensions, coupled with economic crisis, led to the collapse of the federation in 1991, however, and civil war followed as the former constituent countries began declaring their independence. In the following year, Serbia and Montenegro formed what they claimed to be a successor state to Yugoslavia, the Federal Republic of Yugoslavia.

Prior to the formation of Yugoslavia in 1929, nearly all of its constituent states had flown the red, white, and blue Pan-Slavic flag, so in order to distinguish the flag of the newly united Yugoslavia from them, the horizontal order of its stripes was set at blue, white, and red, with the royal arms being added to the center. During the period of communist rule, the arms were replaced by a red, gold-fimbriated "Partisan Star," which was dropped after the federation was dissolved in 1991, Yugoslavia's flag now being left plain.

Capital city:
Beograd (Belgrade)

Location:
Southern Central Europe

Currency:
1 Yugoslav new dinar
= 100 paras

Languages:
Serbian, Albanian, Hungarian

Religions:
Serbian Orthodox, Roman Catholic, Muslim

Flag adopted:
April 27, 1992

Flag ratio:
1:2

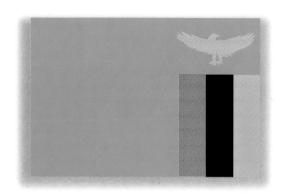

Formal name:
Republic of Zambia

Capital city:
Lusaka

Location:
Southern Africa

Currency:
1 Zambian kwacha
= 100 ngwee

Languages:
English, Bantu

Religions:
Christian, Animist

Flag adopted:
October 24, 1964

Flag ratio:
2:3

The central-southern African region known as Zambia was visited by the Portuguese during the late-18th century, and by the British explorer Dr. David Livingstone in 1851. During the 1890s, the area was under the control of Cecil Rhodes's British South Africa Company. As Northern Rhodesia, it became a British protectorate in 1924, until 1963 forming part of the Federation of Rhodesia and Nyasaland with Southern Rhodesia (now Zimbabwe) and Nyasaland (now Malawi). In 1964, Northern Rhodesia became the independent Republic of Zambia.

At the time of its independence, Zambia's United National Independence Party (U.N.I.P.) was politically dominant, and the party's colors formed the basis of the flag's design. A red, black, and orange horizontally striped tricolor appears on the green field (denoting Zambia's agriculture), the red standing for its struggle for freedom, the black symbolizing its people, and the orange its mineral wealth. Above the tricolor charge is a *Nkwazi* (fish eagle, common to the Zambesi River area), derived from the arms of Zambia, which originally held a fish in its talons. On independence, however, the fish was removed because it was felt that it recalled the colonial rulers' control over Zambia's people. Zambia's flag is unusual in that the charges are situated in the fly half, only being visible when a strong wind blows.

ZIMBABWE

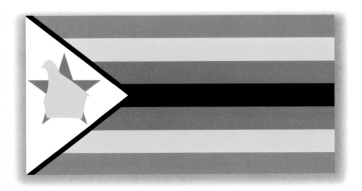

Formal name:
Republic of Zimbabwe

Formerly a British protectorate known as Southern Rhodesia, and then as Rhodesia, in 1980 this southern African country was renamed Zimbabwe after the 14th-century stone city of Great Zimbabwe, in the southeast of the country. (In Bantu, Zimbabwe means "House of Stone.") Following its split from the Federation of Rhodesia and Nyasaland in 1953, African nationalists campaigned for full democracy and independence for Rhodesia. Although Ian Smith's government unilaterally declared Rhodesia an independent republic in 1969, it refused to progress toward a black-majority-rule constitution until 1979. In 1980, following the election to government of the Zimbabwe African National Union-Patriotic Front (Z.A.N.U.-P.F.), Zimbabwe finally became fully independent.

The flag that Zimbabwe adopted on attaining independence was based on the Z.A.N.U. flag, which consisted of concentric panels of green, yellow, and red arranged around a central black stripe. As well as being Pan-African colors, in Zimbabwe's flag, the green represents the land, the yellow its mineral wealth, the red the blood of the people, and the black the country's black majority. The white triangle in the hoist, which signifies both peace and "the way forward," contains Zimbabwe's national emblem, a bird carved in soapstone (such as those found at the ruined city of Great Zimbabwe) superimposed on a red star, which symbolizes the international outlook of the country.

Capital city:
Harare

Location:
Southern Africa

Currency:
1 Zimbabwe dollar = 100 cents

Languages
English, Bantu

Religions:
Christian, Animist

Flag adopted:
April 18, 1980

Flag ratio:
1:2

The following internationally recognized flags belong to nonpolitical organizations and political groupings.

Formal name:
League of Arab States

Status:
grouping

Headquarters:
Cairo, Egypt

Language:
Arabic

The Arab League was founded in 1945 to promote economic and cultural links and minimize conflicts between Arab states.

The green of the flag's field is the traditional color of the Prophet Muhammad. The crescent emblem cradles the *shahada* (statement of Islamic faith), while the chain and laurel leaves symbolize the Arab states united in peace.

ASSOCIATION OF SOUTHEAST ASIAN NATIONS (A.S.E.A.N.)

Status:
grouping

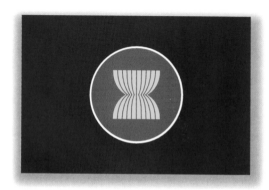

The Association of Southeast Asian Nations was established in 1967 by Indonesia, Malaysia, Singapore, the Philippines, and Thailand to promote mutual economic development.

The blue field of the flag symbolizes peace and stability, while the central red disk, denoting courage and dynamism, is fimbriated with white, representing purity. The yellow motif (symbolizing prosperity) is of a rice sheaf with ten stalks, one for each of the current member states.

CARIBBEAN COMMUNITY (CARICOM)

Status:
grouping

Founded in 1973, the Caribbean Community is an organization made up of former British colonies in the Caribbean whose aim is to promote cooperation in economic, cultural, and technological matters, as well as coordinating a common foreign policy.

The light and dark blues of the flag represent the sky and sea. The yellow disk denotes the sun, while the black letters are the initials of the group's full name.

COMMONWEALTH

Status:
grouping

Headquarters:
London, U.K.

Languages:
English, French, Portuguese

The Commonwealth is an informal grouping comprising the United Kingdom and the majority of its former dependencies. The Commonwealth has no charter or constitution, but the heads of the governments that belong to it meet every two years. The origins of the Commonwealth lie in the 1926 Imperial Conference, which defined the dominions of the British Empire as freely associated members of the British Commonwealth of Nations. Its member states, while independent in every respect, recognize the British monarch as head of the Commonwealth.

The Commonwealth flag depicts a stylized globe surrounded by radiating lines that form the letter "C" (for Commonwealth). Although it was originally intended that each member state should be represented by a ray-like line, this was eventually deemed impractical.

COMMONWEALTH OF INDEPENDENT STATES (C.I.S.)

Status:
grouping

Headquarters:
Minsk, Belarus

Language:
Russian

Formally established in 1992, the Commonwealth of Independent States (C.I.S.) is an organization of some, but not all, of the former members of the U.S.S.R. Although its member states function independently, the C.I.S. was granted some authority for establishing and maintaining economic, political, and military coordination, along with environmental protection and crime-fighting.

The flag of the C.I.S., which is said to represent a vigorous tree, symbolizes cooperation. The blue field denotes the sky, and the yellow disk, the sun.

EUROPEAN UNION (E.U.)

Status:
grouping

Headquarters:
Brussels, Belgium

Languages:
English, French, German, Greek

The European Union (E.U.) came into being as a result of the terms of the Treaty of Maastricht of 1991. On November 1, 1993, the former European Community (E.C.), formed from the European Economic Community (E.E.C.), and Euratom, the European Atomic Energy Community, which was formed in 1957 according to the terms of the Treaty of Rome, were absorbed into the European Union. As defined by the Treaty of Maastricht, the E.U. is the expression of "an even closer union among the peoples of Europe." The governments of the 12 E.C. member states that ratified this treaty agreed a series of common objectives, including, eventually, a single currency (the euro). Every citizen of an E.U. member state is also a citizen of the E.U., with the right to reside, work, vote, and stand for election to local and regional government authorities in any E.U. member country.

The twelve stars that are arranged on the E.U.'s flag indicate completeness and union rather than the actual number of member countries (there are currently 15). When flown with a member state's flag, the E.U.'s flag takes the position of honor. The E.U.'s flag is the same as the flag of the Council of Europe (which has 25 member states), which aims to safeguard the common European heritage and protect human rights.

NORTH ATLANTIC TREATY ORGANIZATION (N.A.T.O.)

Status:
grouping

Headquarters:
Brussels, Belgium (headquarters of the international secretariat), Chièvres, near Mons, Belgium (Supreme Headquarters Allied Powers Europe (S.H.A.P.E.), the military headquarters)

Languages:
English, French

The North Atlantic Treaty Organization (N.A.T.O.) was set up in 1949 to provide for the collective defense of the major European and North American states against the then perceived threat of the U.S.S.R., members pledging each other assistance in the event of armed aggression against them. The original members were Belgium, Canada, Denmark, France, Iceland, Italy, Luxembourg, the Netherlands, Norway, Portugal, the U.K., and the U.S. Greece, Turkey, Germany (which joined in 1955 as West Germany before being reunified with East Germany in 1990), and Spain joined later. Following the dissolution of the Eastern European Warsaw Pact in 1991, an adjunct to N.A.T.O., the North Atlantic Cooperation Council, was established, which included former Soviet republics and Eastern bloc countries and aimed to achieve greater European security.

The blue field of N.A.T.O.'s flag represents the Atlantic Ocean. The compass rose, which points north, south, east, and west, symbolically points to the member states on either side of the Atlantic.

Formal name:
International Olympic
Committee

Status:
international organization

Languages:
English, French

The Olympic Games, the greatest festival of Ancient Greece, were held every four years on the plain of Olympia, in Elis, in honor of the supreme Greek god, Zeus. The concept of an international sporting event in the form of the Modern Olympic Games was revived during the late 19th century.

Although the design of the Olympic flag was adopted in 1913, it was first flown at the 1920 Olympic Games in Antwerp, Belgium. The five rings represent the harmonious joining of the five continents of Africa, America, Asia, Europe, and Oceania. At least one of the colors of the Olympic rings appears in the flag of every country in the world.

ORGANIZATION OF AFRICAN UNITY (O.A.U.)

Status:
grouping

Headquarters:
Addis Ababa, Ethiopia

Languages:
English, French, Arabic,
Portuguese

The Organization of African Unity (O.A.U.), an association of African states, was established in 1963 to eradicate colonialism and foster economic, cultural, and political cooperation.

The green stripes of the O.A.U.'s flag represent the forests and grasslands of the continent, while the orange symbolizes the deserts and the central white stripe denotes peace and cooperation. The flag is charged with a central emblem depicting a green-encircled silhouette of Africa, cradled within yellow, green, and red stylized horns.

ORGANIZATION OF AMERICAN STATES (O.A.S.)

Status:
grouping

Languages:
English, French, Spanish,
Portuguese

In 1948, a charter signed by thirty representatives of Northern, Central, and Southern American states founded the Organization of American States (O.A.S.), which aims to maintain peace and unity in the western hemisphere. It also concerns itself with the social and economic development of Latin America.

The central motif of the organization's flag is made up of the national colors of each of the member states, of which there are now thirty-five.

ORGANIZATION OF PETROLEUM EXPORTING COUNTRIES (O.P.E.C.)

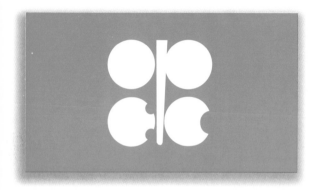

Status:
grouping

Languages:
English, Arabic

The Organization of Petroleum Exporting Countries (O.P.E.C.) was established in 1960 to coordinate the price-and-supply policies of oil-producing states and to improve the position of Third World countries by urging richer nations to open up their markets to their products.

O.P.E.C.'s flag, which was adopted during the 1970s, uses colors similar to those that appear on the flag of the United Nations. The central white emblem is a stylized version of the agency's initials.

PACIFIC COMMUNITY

Status:
Grouping

Headquarters:
Noumea, New Caledonia

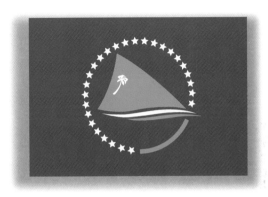

The Pacific Coummunity includes independent states that are situated in Oceana, as well as overseas dependencies and colonies of the United States of America, the United Kingdom, Australia, France, and New Zealand. The association works to protect and foster the economic, cultural, political and environmental security of its 27 members.

RED CROSS
and RED CRESCENT

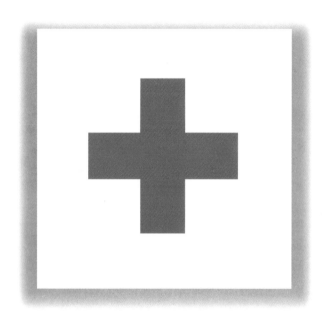

The International Committee of the Red Cross (I.C.R.C.), an international relief agency, was founded by the Geneva Convention of 1864 at the instigation of a Swiss doctor, Henry Dunant, to assist the wounded and prisoners of war.

The emblem that the I.C.R.C. adopted was a red cross on a white field (a transposition of the colors and couped cross of the flag of Switzerland, a country that has consistently maintained its neutrality), which is known as the "Red Cross."

In 1876, however, during the Russo-Turkish War, the Muslim Ottoman Empire decided to use a red crescent on a white field instead of the cross, whose symbolism is Christian. Egypt also adopted the "Red Crescent," while Persia opted for a red lion and sun on a white field. Both emblems were formally incorporated into the Geneva Convention of 1929. Although the lion-and-sun flag has not been used since 1980, when the Islamic Republic of Iran (formerly Persia) began using the Red Crescent, under the Geneva Convention it remains a recognized and protected symbol, whose misuse is condemned as a war crime (as, indeed, is the misuse of the Red Cross or Red Crescent).

Because the I.C.R.C. is increasingly concerned with aiding victims of natural disasters, such as floods, epidemics, and earthquakes, a new, culturally neutral symbol called the "Red Chevron" is being considered.

Formal name:
International Committee of the Red Cross (I.C.R.C.)

Status:
international organization

Headquarters:
Geneva, Switzerland

UNITED NATIONS (U.N.)

Status:
grouping

Headquarters:
New York, N.Y., U.S.

Languages:
English, French

The United Nations (U.N.) was established in New York in 1945 to act as a successor to the League of Nations (formed in Geneva, Switzerland, in 1920).

The name 'United Nations' was coined by U.S. President F. D. Roosevelt, and its founder members were the United States, the U.K., and the U.S.S.R., which charged the U.N. with three basic functions: to maintain international peace and security; to develop friendly and equal relations among nations; and to encourage international cooperation in solving international problems of a social, cultural, or humanitarian nature. It was also given the authority to discuss and make recommendations in order to settle disputes and, if necessary, to take measures to enforce peace. Other important agencies of the U.N. include the Permanent Court of International Justice (in The Hague, the Netherlands), the World Bank, the International Monetary Fund (I.M.F.), and the World Health Organization (W.H.O.).

The blue-and-white flag of the United Nations – one of the most recognized international flags – depicts the world as seen on a map, with its center at the North Pole, surrounded by the ancient symbol of peace: an olive wreath.

ALABAMA

State Capital: Montgomery   Joined Union: 1819   Flag Adopted: 1895

The red saltire on a white field recalls the "Flag of the South," the Battle Flag of the Confederate States (1861). Alabama, the 22nd state of the Union, was one of the original seven states to secede from it in February 1861 to form the rebel Confederate States of America.

ALASKA

State Capital: Juneau   Joined Union: 1959   Flag Adopted 1926

The 49th state of the United States, Alaska's flag was designed when it was still a territory. The golden stars on a blue field depict the constellation of the Plough and the northern Pole star.

ARIZONA

State Capital: Phoenix   Joined Union: 1912   Flag Adopted: 1927

The central copper star represents Arizona's rich mineral resources, while the red and yellow stripes evoke the sun's rays while recalling the 48th state's period of Spanish rule.

ARKANSAS

State Capital: Little Rock   Joined Union: 1836   Flag Adopted: 1913

A variation on the design of the "The Flag of the South," the three, blue, lower stars beneath the state name represent the former colonial powers while the upper star stands for the Confederacy, which Arkansas joined in 1861.

CALIFORNIA

State Capital: Sacramento   Joined Union: 1850 Flag Adopted: 1911

Depicting a grizzly bear and star of freedom, California's flag was based on the flag of the Republic of California which declared independence from Mexico in 1846 at Sonoro.

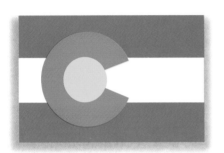

COLORADO

State Capital: Denver Joined Union: 1876   Flag Adopted: 1911

Colorado entered the Union as the 38th state. The red "C" of Colorado surrounding a golden disc recalls the region's Spanish heritage and refer to the state's mineral resources.

CONNECTICUT

State Capital: Hartford   Joined Union: 1788   Flag Adopted: 1897

Connecticut's flag bears the state arms which date back to the seal of 1784. The blue field of the flag, a Union color, dates from the Civil War of 1861-85.

DELAWARE

State Capital: Dover   Joined Union: 1787   Flag Adopted: 1913

Delaware's flag bears the state arms which date back to 1777 and the flag includes the date on which the state joined the Union. The colors of the flag also recall the uniforms worn in the American Revolution.

FEDERAL DISTRICT OF COLUMBIA

Joined Union: 1791   Flag Adopted: 1938

The District of Columbia is a federal area that is coextensive with the federal capital, Washington, and is governed by Congress. The flag is based on a banner which dates back to 1592 belonging to the family of the first President of the United States, George Washington.

FLORIDA

State Capital: Tallahassee   Joined Union: 1845   Flag Adopted: 1900

The 27th state to join the Union, Florida's original flag which it adopted in 1868, only bore the great seal. The red saltire, recalling the "Flag of the South" and Florida's part in the Confederacy, was added in 1900.

GEORGIA

State Capital: Atlanta   Joined Union: 1788   Flag Adopted: 2001

Georgia has flown many flags in its history including the "Stars and Bars" flag of the Confederacy and the "Southern Cross" Battle Flag, as its present flag demonstrates. The state seal bears the date of 1776, the year of the Declaration of Independence, and depicts a soldier with a drawn sword ready to defend the nation and its principles.

HAWAII

State Capital: Honolulu   Joined Union: 1959   Flag Adopted: 1845

An independent kingdom until 1893, Hawaii became a republic in 1894, ceded itself to the United States in 1898, became a U.S. Territory in 1900 and the 50th state of the Union in 1959. The eight stripes represent the main islands of Nihau, Kauai, Oahu, Molokai, Lanai, Maui, Kahoolawe, and Hawaii. The Union Jack in the canton recalls the flag given to the Hawaiian king by a British army officer in 1793.

IDAHO

State Capital: Boise   Joined Union: 1890   Flag Adopted: 1927

The flag of Idaho, the 43rd state to join the Union, was originally a military banner. Today it bears the great seal of the state depicting a farmer and a soldier, beneath which is a scroll with the state's name.

ILLINOIS

State Capital: Springfield   Joined Union: 1818   Flag Adopted: 1970

The 21st state of the Union, Illinois's state flag was first designed in 1915 and uses the emblems of a bald eagle and shield of the Stars and Stripes drawn from the state seal. In 1970, the state's name was added to the flag.

INDIANA

State Capital: Indianapolis   Joined Union: 1816   Flag Adopted: 1917

The design of Indiana's flag was the winner in a competition held in 1916. A central flaming torch, above which is the state name, is surrounded by 19 golden stars – one for each of the other states in the Union when Indiana joined in 1816 as the 19th state.

IOWA

State Capital: Des Moines   Joined Union: 1846   Flag Adopted: 1921

Iowa, the 29th state of the Union, was once part of French Louisiana and the red, white, and blue of the flag recalls the state's history. In the central white stripe is a bald-headed eagle carrying a scroll on which is written the state motto: "Our liberties we prize and our rights we will maintain." The Iowa state flag in this form dates from 1921.

KANSAS

State Capital: Topeka   Joined Union: 1861   Flag Adopted: 1963

The 34th state to join the Union, the original flag of Kansas dates from 1925 and bore the state seal depicting a farmer ploughing in front of a homestead. It was also charged with a sunflower, the state flower, which today, appears above the seal. In 1963, the state name was added to the flag.

KENTUCKY

State Capital: Frankfort   Joined Union: 1792   Flag Adopted: 1918

The 15th state of the Union, Kentucky's flag, like many other state flags, bears the state seal and name. The seal depicts two figures around which are the words: "United we stand divided we fall," and is surrounded by a wreath of the state flower, golden rod.

LOUISIANA

State Capital: Baton Rouge   Joined Union: 1812   Flag Adopted: 1912

In 1803, territory extending from the Mississippi River to the Rocky Mountains and from the Gulf of Mexico to Canada was purchased by the United States for $15 million from France. Part of this purchase was land that became Louisiana, the 18th state of the Union, whose emblem is the pelican, said to pluck its breast so its offspring may prosper.

MAINE

State Capital: Augusta   Joined Union: 1820   Flag Adopted: 1909

When Maine joined the Union in 1820 as the 23rd state, it was the northernmost state, a fact recalled in the flag by the shining Pole star and the motto "Dirigo" (Latin: to lead, or, show the way). A farmer and a sailor, recalling the state's main interests, support a shield bearing a deer beneath a pine tree. In 1909, these arms were placed onto the blue field to create the state flag.

MARYLAND

State Capital: Annapolis   Joined Union: 1788   Flag Adopted: 1904

Maryland's flag is unique among the state flags in that it is the only one which is a heraldic banner. It bears the arms of Sir George Calvert, 1st Baron Baltimore, an English politician and founder of the colony of Maryland, whose descendants were the colonial rulers until the American Revolution.

MASSACHUSETTS

State Capital: Boston   Joined Union: 1788   Flag Adopted: 1971

The arms of Massachusetts date from 1780 and depict a Native American holding a bow. The arms were added to both sides of the state flag in 1971, replacing the emblem of a pine tree that had been in use since 1908.

MICHIGAN

State Capital: Lansing   Joined Union: 1837   Flag Adopted: 1911

The arms of Michigan, the 26th state of the Union, which appear on plain blue field, were adopted in 1832. Beneath the shield, the motto reads "If you seek a pleasant peninsula, look about you." The figure bearing a rifle stands at the edge of the great lake. Above him the legend reads: "I will defend."

MINNESOTA

State Capital: St. Paul   Joined Union: 1858   Flag Adopted: 1893

When Minnesota joined the Union in 1858 as the 32nd state, it also became the northernmost state, which is reflected in the motto on the state flag which reads: "L'Etoile du Nord" (North Star).

MISSISSIPPI

State Capital: Jackson   Joined Union: 1817   Flag Adopted: 1894

The 20th state of the Union, Mississippi's flag recalls the state's historic past during the American Civil War and combines the "Stars and Bars" flag of the Confederacy (although on Mississippi's flag the order of the red and blue stripes is transposed) with the "Battle Flag of the South" that makes the canton.

MISSOURI

State Capital: Jefferson City   Joined Union: 1821   Flag Adopted: 1913

Missouri became the 24th state to join the Union and this fact is proudly reflected in the 24 stars surrounding the state seal (which also displays the same number of stars). Before joining, Missouri was French territory, and this part of its history can be seen in the use of a horizontal *tricolore* field.

MONTANA

State Capital: Helena   Joined Union: 1889   Flag Adopted: 1905

Spain once claimed this territory: the state motto "Gold and Silver" is in Spanish and the emblem depicts a mining scene beside a river. Two mighty rivers – the Yellowstone and the Missouri – flow through the 41st state of the Union. In 1981 the design was revised to include the state name.

NEBRASKA

State Capital: Lincoln   Joined Union: 1867   Flag Adopted: 1925

The 37th state to enter the Union, Nebraska's flag is another flag that bears the great seal of the state which was adopted in 1867. The seal depicts a blacksmith working with a hammer and anvil situated in an agricultural landscape while the motto reads: "Equality Before the Land."

NEVADA

State Capital: Carson City   **Joined Union:** 1864   **Flag Adopted:** 1929

Sage bush and the star are the emblems of the 36th state of the Union and these found themselves on the winning design in the state flag competition held in 1929. The motto proudly declares "Battle Born." In 1991 the state name was added to the design.

NEW HAMPSHIRE

State Capital: Concord   **Joined Union:** 1788   **Flag Adopted:** 1909

The design of New Hampshire's flag is based on the great state seal which dates from 1776. The seal depicts the ship the *Raleigh* being built at the town of Portsmouth, on the Atlantic coast during the American Revolution.

NEW JERSEY

State Capital: Trenton   **Joined Union:** 1787   **Flag Adopted:** 1896

The arms of New Jersey contain a shield bearing three ploughshares. Two maidens, one with a staff and a red cap of liberty, another with a "horn of plenty." are the supporters. The buff color of the field recalls the colors of the uniforms worn during the American Revolution.

NEW MEXICO

State Capital: Santa Fe   **Joined Union:** 1912   **Flag Adopted:** 1925

New Mexico was the 47th state to enter the Union and reflecting the Native American culture of the region, the distinctive state flag uses the sun symbol of the Zia Pueblo Indians.

NEW YORK

State Capital: Albany   Joined Union: 1788   Flag Adopted: 1901

New York's flag is based on forms used during the American Revolution and before 1901, the field was the plain buff color of the uniforms of the Revolutionary Army. The two female supporters represent Liberty (with the cap and staff) and Justice (blindfolded and holding the weighing scales). In the shield, two ships – one merchant and one pleasure craft – sail the Hudson River against the backdrop of the Catskill Mountains.

NORTH CAROLINA

State Capital: Raleigh   Joined Union: 1789   Flag Adopted: 1885

North Carolina's original flag dated from the outbreak of the American Civil War in 1861. The present design, a variation of the "Stars and Bars" flag of the Confederacy, dates from 1885 and bears the state's initials.

NORTH DAKOTA

State Capital: Bismarck   Joined Union: 1889   Flag Adopted: 1911

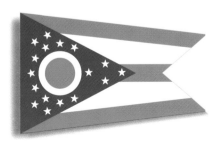

The 39th state of the Union, North Dakota is unusual in that its state flag is square in shape because it was originally a military banner born by the state militia, the North Dakota Infantry. In the center of the flag is a version of the national arms of the United States of America.

OHIO

State Capital: Columbus   Joined Union: 1803   Flag Adopted 1803

Ohio's state flag is a pennant-shaped flag whose origins lay in a cavalry *guidon* (a signal flag) of the Civil War. The 17th state to join the Union, Ohio's flag proudly recalls this in the 17 stars surrounding the letter "O" of the state's initial.

OKLAHOMA

State Capital: Oklahoma City   Joined Union: 1907   Flag Adopted: 1941.

Oklahoma was the 46th state to join the Union and its state flag recalls its history and previous name of "Indian Territory." The result of a design competition in 1925, the state name was added in 1941 beneath the central Native American emblems which are symbols of peace.

OREGON

State Capital: Salem   Joined Union: 1859   Flag Adopted: 1925

Oregon's flag is unique in that it is the only state flag to have a different design on the reverse side. The obverse (front) bears the state seal, the state name and 33 stars recalling the fact that Oregon was the 33rd state to join the Union in 1859. The reverse side depicts the state animal, the beaver.

PENNSYLVANIA

State Capital: Harrisburg   Joined Union: 1787   Flag Adopted: 1907

Pennsylvania's flag bears the coat of arms of the state which was adopted in 1777. Surmounted by an American eagle, the shield is supported by two black horses whose hooves stand on a scroll bearing the state motto: "Virtue, Liberty, and Independence." In was in Philadelphia, Pennsylvania, on 4 July 1776, that the Declaration of Independence was signed.

RHODE ISLAND

State Capital: Providence   Joined Union: 1790   Flag Adopted: 1877

The smallest state in the Union, Rhode Island, was one of the original 13 colonies to rebel against British rule and declare independence. Its square-shaped flag, based on a Revolutionary standard, is charged with the emblem of hope, an anchor.

SOUTH CAROLINA

State Capital: Columbia   Joined Union: 1788   Flag Adopted: 1861

South Carolina's flag contains emblems used during the Revolutionary War, but the flag itself was adopted at the start of the Civil War. The central tree emblem gives the state its nickname as the Palmetto State.

SOUTH DAKOTA

State Capital: Pierre   Joined Union: 1889   Flag Adopted: 1963

The 40th state to enter the Union, South Dakota was known as the "Sunshine State" and this legend appeared around the central state seal emblem until 1992 when it was changed to "The Mount Rushmore State."

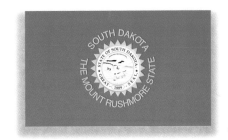

TENNESSEE

State Capital: Nashville   Joined Union: 1796   Flag Adopted: 1905

After the 13 colonies had declared their independence from British rule, Tennessee became the third state to join the Union and this is reflected in the three stars on the state flag. Drawing on the "Stars and Bars" design, the flag is also a reminder that Tennessee was one of the 10 states to secede from the Union in 1862.

TEXAS

State Capital: Austin   Joined Union: 1845   Flag Adopted: 1839

Texas adopted its state flag some six years before it joined the Union as the 28th state in 1845. It uses the colors of the "Stars and Stripes" but only one star – hence its nickname, "The Lone Star State." A single star was also used on a plain blue field during the time of the Republic of Texas from 1836-1845.

UTAH

State Capital: Salt Lake City   Joined Union: 1896   Flag Adopted: 1911

When Utah became the 45th state of the Union in 1896, it adopted its state seal which bears the emblem of a beehive and the date 1847. These recall the date of the Mormon settlement of the region and the establishment of the Mormon state of Deseret in Utah.

VERMONT

State Capital: Montpelier   Joined Union: 1791   Flag Adopted: 1923

Before becoming the 14th state of the Union, from 1777-1791, Vermont was independent. Known as the "Lone Pine State," this emblem features in the arms of Vermont which appear on the flag. Beneath the shield, on a scroll, is the state's name.

VIRGINIA

State Capital: Richmond   Joined Union: 1788   Flag Adopted: 1861

One of the original rebellious colonies that founded the United Sates of America, Virginia was also one of the ten states that seceded from the Union in 1861 at the start of the Civil War. The state seal bearing a valiant warrior and the state name was placed on the blue field in 1861 to make the state flag.

WASHINGTON

State Capital: Olympia   Joined Union: 1889   Flag Adopted: 1923

The "Evergreen State," Washington was the 42nd state to join the Union and is the only state to have a green flag. The state seal, bearing a portrait bust of the first U.S. President, George Washington (1732-1799) dates from 1889 and was added to the flag in 1923.

WEST VIRGINIA

State Capital: Charleston   Joined Union: 1863   Flag Adopted: 1929

In 1863, West Virginia seceded from Virginia (which had joined the Confederacy) and became the 35th state to join the Union. The state flag adopted in 1929 makes use of the state seal which bears the figures of a farmer and a soldier. Surrounding the shield is a wreath of rhododendrons, the state flower.

WISCONSIN

State Capital: Madison   Joined Union: 1848   Flag Adopted: 1980

Using the state seal of the 30th state of the Union as its arms, the quartered shield is charged with emblems of industry, agriculture, and seafaring and is supported by the figures of a sailor and a miner. Based on the militia colors of the Union in 1863, Wisconsin's name and the date were added in 1980.

WYOMING

State Capital: Cheyenne   Joined Union: 1890   Flag Adopted: 1917

Wyoming's state flag in the red, white, and blue of the national flag, was the result of a design competition held in 1917. Since then, the design has been modified: at one time, the silhouette of the bison containing the great seal of the state was positioned to face the fly.

ALBERTA

Capital: Edmonton   Joined Confederation: 1905   Flag Adopted: 1967

Alberta (along with Saskatchewan) was a province created from the Northwest Territories in 1905. The central shield on Alberta's flag depicts a scene of the wheat fields of the western province under a St. George's cross.

BRITISH COLUMBIA

Capital: Victoria   Joined Confederation: 1871   Flag Adopted: 1960

British Columbia joined the Dominion of Canada in 1871. The flag is an armorial banner of the arms granted to the province in 1906 and bears the emblem of a blazing sun over water and symbolizes the province's western location on the shores of the Pacific Ocean.

MANITOBA

Capital: Winnipeg   Joined Confederation: 1870   Flag Adopted: 1966

This central Canadian province used the Canadian Red Ensign as the basis for its flag. In place of the quartered shield bearing the emblems of England, France, Scotland, and Ireland, the provincial flag is charged with the arms of Manitoba, depicting a buffalo standing on a rock.

NEW BRUNSWICK

Capital: Fredericton   Joined Confederation: 1867   Flag adopted: 1965

Like British Columbia, New Brunswick's flag is an armorial banner. The galley ship recalls the industry that once dominated the south-eastern province that borders the U.S. state of Maine. The lion in the upper third symbolizes New Brunswick's historical ties with Britain.

NEWFOUNDLAND AND LABRADOR

Capital: St. John's   Joined Confederation: 1949

Part of French-speaking Lower Canada in 1791, which joined with Upper Canada in 1841 to form Canada Province, the flag of the province recalls the design of the British Union Jack. The colors were intended to symbolize the ice, snow and the sea of the north-eastern province.

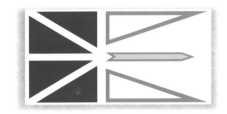

NORTHWEST TERRITORIES

Joined Confederation: 1870   Flag Adopted: 1969

The Northwest Territories lies to the north of the Canadian provinces and extends east from Yukon Territory to the Davis Strait. The flag bears the arms granted in 1956. The colors of the field symbolize the lakes and rivers (blue) and the snow (white).

NOVA SCOTIA

Capital: Halifax   Joined Confederation: 1867   Flag Adopted: uncertain

Nova Scotia means 'New Scotland' and its is believed to be the oldest flag of a British Dominion. It uses the cross of Scotland's patron saint Andrew (with the colors reversed – in the Union Jack it is white on blue) with the Scottish Royal arms of a lion *rampant*.

ONTARIO

Capital: Toronto   Joined Confederation: 1867   Flag Adopted: 1965

The southern province of Ontario borders the Great Lakes and made up much of English-speaking Upper Canada in 1791. The flag is based on the Canadian Red Ensign but uses a shield taken from the arms granted in 1868 in which, the maple-leaf emblem appeared for the first time.

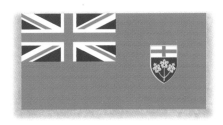

PRINCE EDWARD ISLAND

Capital: Charlottetown   Joined Confederation: 1873   Flag Adopted: 1905

Another armorial banner, the flag of province of Prince Edward Island, which lies in the Gulf of the St. Lawrence River, uses the arms granted in 1905. It depicts an island on which a mighty oak tree and its young seedlings are symbolically protected by the lion of Britain.

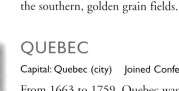

SASKATCHEWAN

Capital: Regina   Joined Confederation: 1905   Flag Adopted: 1969

The flag of the western Canadian province of Saskatchewan incorporates the arms of three wheat sheaves, the British lion and the flower emblem of the province, the beautiful western red lily. The bicolored field symbolizes the green, northern forests and the southern, golden grain fields.

QUEBEC

Capital: Quebec (city)   Joined Confederation: 1867   Flag Adopted: 1948

From 1663 to 1759, Quebec was called New France until it was taken by the British. Part of French-speaking Lower Canada from 1791, the eastern province of Quebec was united with Upper Quebec in 1841 when the self-governing Dominion of Canada was formed. It's famous provincial flag bears testament to the French heritage in its use of the *fleur-de-lis* emblem of France.

YUKON TERRITORY

Capital: Whitehorse   Joined Confederation: 1898   Flag Adopted: 1967

The vast, north-western Canadian territory of Yukon was the location for the famous Klondike gold rush of 1897-98. The territory's flag makes use of the arms adopted in 1956. Proudly standing atop the shield is a Husky, famous for their sled-pulling abilities. The colors symbolize the forests (green), the winter snows (white), and the clear waters of the lakes, rivers and seas (blue).